Thr

Generations of Suffering

Three Generations of Suffering

A Chronicle of One Family's Persecution in an Atheistic Society

Georgi Vins

Translated by Jane Ellis

Lighthouse Trails Publishing
Roseburg, Oregon

Three Generations of Suffering
Second Edition 2022 by Lighthouse Trails Publishing
(see back of book for publisher and author contact information)

 Scripture quotations are taken from the *King James Version* unless otherwise indicated.

Cover and interior design by Lighthouse Trails Publishing. Cover photos from Georgi Vins' family collection; used with permission.

First published in 1975 by David C. Cook Publishing Co. as *Georgi Vins: Prisoner of Conscience* and also titled *Testament From Prison* (ISBN: 0-912692-84-7); also published in 1976, 1979 as *Three Generations of Suffering* by Hodder and Stroughton (ISBN: 0-34020417-6 and 0-34025023-2). Rights held by Georgi Vins family; used with permission. For photo credits, see page 223.

Publisher's Cataloging-in-Publication Data
Vins, G. P. (Georgi Petrovich), 1928-1998
Three generations of suffering: an autobiography of Christian persecution in the U.S.S.R. / Georgi Vins. -- Lighthouse Trails Edition.
224 pages cm
Includes bibliographical references and index.
ISBN: 978-1-942423-59-1 (softbound : alk. paper) 1. Vins, G. P. (Georgi Petrovich), 1928-1998 2. Baptists--Russia--Biography. I. Title.

Library of Congress Control Number: 2022941790

Note: Lighthouse Trails Publishing books are available at special quantity discounts. Contact information for publisher in back of book.

Printed in the United States of America

CONTENTS

There is no question of justice. Atheism, invested with power, creates tyranny.

— **Georgi Vins**

INTRODUCTION

Introduction written in 1975
by Jane Ellis, the translator of this book

> We require that religion should be a private matter as far as the state is concerned. The state must have nothing to do with religion. Religious societies must not be connected with the state power. Religious and church societies must be completely free unions of like-minded citizens independent of the authorities.
> (V. I. Lenin, Socialism and Religion)

Not a vestige of this ideal of Lenin remains in Soviet life. In this book, Georgi Vins shows what a travesty has been made of it. Religion in the Soviet Union is very far from being "a private matter." It is subject to laws limiting its freedom. It is the target of state-backed atheist propaganda. The churches are under the thumb of state organizations set up to control them. Believers are victims of illegal suppression.

All this is vividly illustrated by Georgi Vin's two essays, which describe the lives of a number of Soviet believers. The first, "A Family Chronicle," is about his own family which for forty-five years has suffered bitterly for its Christian faith. It is by no means exceptional: Georgi Vins prefaces the tale of its hardships with the words, "This is an ordinary chronicle of a normal Christian family, one of the many thousands in our country." There are three generations of suffering in this "normal" family. Peter Vin died in a labor camp in 1943, but his wife, Lydia, has recently survived a prison sentence and still lives in Kiev. Their son, Georgi, the author of this book, has suffered imprisonment and harassment by the police, so that the burden of worrying about him and caring for the family has fallen on the shoulders of his wife, Nadezhda.

Now discrimination at work is the lot of the third generation, Georgi and Nadezhda's children: their eldest daughter Natasha, their son Petya, the two younger girls, Liza and Zhenya, and the baby, Alexander.

The second essay, "Faithful Servants of God,"* consists of short biographies of a number of leading Russian Baptists in the twentieth century. Extracts from their letters, sermons, and articles are included. This essay is a mine of information about the lives of believers in the capital of Moscow and in remote villages, in the central offices of the Baptist Union, and in small communities in the Far East and Siberia. It shows how their lives were at the mercy of fluctuations of state policy: how eagerly they seized the opportunity to preach the Gospel in the breathing-space just after the Revolution, and how with the beginning of persecution in 1929 many of them were led off to prisons and labor camps and few returned. It is a testimony to the faith and courage of men and women who morning by morning faced the bleak reality of treading the thorny path of Christ through the frozen wastelands of Soviet labor camps. Fragmentary though it is, "Faithful Servants of God" provides many new glimpses into the history of suffering of Soviet Baptists.

The term "Baptist" in the Soviet Union is commonly, though loosely, used to refer to a member of the Evangelical Christian-Baptist (ECB) Church. This is the official name of the church formed by the amalgamation of the Evangelical Christians with the Baptists under the Soviet regime. The official governing body of the church is the All-Union Council of Evangelical Christians-Baptists (AUCECB). Since the beginning of the 1960s, Georgi Vins has been a leader of opposition to the policies of the All-Union Council. Soviet atheists called the opposition movement the *Initsiativniki,* but we usually refer to them as "Reform Baptists."**

---

*This edition has divided the second essay into two parts, the second being "Faithful Christian Women." **This term is not affiliated with Reformed Theology or Calvinism.

They are unable to register their churches—or prayer houses, as they usually call them—with the state authorities. A church in the Soviet Union cannot legally function without being registered by the state, one of the key instances of state interference in the "private matter" of religion. So the Reform Baptists are driven to meet for worship illegally, in private houses or out in the forests, and this frequently leads to the breaking up of meetings, arrests, fines, and imprisonment. Since 1961, there have usually been about two hundred Reform Baptists in prison at any one time.

Despite some reports of local acts of reconciliation in recent years, there is still strong feeling on both sides of the Baptist schism. Georgi Vins has some very sharp comments to make about the All-Union Council, believing that they have betrayed the ideals for which he and his family have suffered. The statements he makes are spawned by his personal experiences.

The story of the formation of the All-Union Council of Evangelical Christians-Baptists, and the rise of opposition to it within the church, can be found in *Faith on Trial in Russia,* * by Michael Bourdeaux, Hodder & Stoughton, 1971. It is also a (partial) biography of Georgi Vins**

The story of the Vins family given in "A Family Chronicle" is considerably expanded by a number of documents in the archives of Keston College (the Centre for the Study of Religion and Communism). These documents have been sent to the West by a group within the Reform Baptists, called the Council of Prisoners' Relatives. One of its presidents was Lydia Vins, who carried through the remarkable work of assembling and sending abroad detailed information about Reform Baptist prisoners. From these documents, we can construct the following history of the Vins family. It is a story which is continuing even as it is written, for Georgi Vins is now in prison for the second time, and his fate is far from certain.

---

* Used copies of this book are available on Amazon. **Also see *The Gospel in Bonds* and *Moscow Express* by Georgi Vins (Lighthouse Trails).

Peter Vins, Georgi's father, of German origin, came from Samara (now Kuibyshev). As a young man, he went to America for theological education not available in Russia and spent his time there first at Weston Memorial Baptist Church in Philadelphia, then at the Colgate-Rochester Divinity School in Rochester, New York, and from 1919-1922 at the Southern Baptist Seminary at Louisville, Kentucky. On his return to the Soviet Union in the spring of 1922, he went to Siberia as a missionary. From that time on, he was an active and wholehearted member of the Baptist Church in the Soviet Union. From 1926-1930, he served as pastor in Blagoveshchensk-on-Amur in the Far East.

Georgi Vins describes his father's three arrests in the "Chronicle." The first arrest led to a labor camp sentence, but at the trial following his second arrest Vins and his eleven co-defendants were, surprisingly, acquitted. It is surprising because it happened at the end of 1936 during Stalin's Great Terror when all over the Soviet Union innocent people were being swept into the prisons and labor camps, never to return. After his third and final arrest, there was no news of Peter Vins for many years. Eventually, his family learned that he had died in a labor camp in the Far East. A full account of the last fifteen years of his life is provided here for the first time by his son.

Like his father, Georgi Vins (born in 1928) was an active member of the Baptist Church, and he also became a pastor. He received a higher education and holds two degrees, one in economics and one in engineering. Nothing is known of his Christian activities before he emerged as one of the leaders of the Reform Baptists. This began in 1960 with the publication by the All-Union Council of the "Letter of Instructions" and the "New Statutes," which in Vins' opinion threatened to give the state the means of suffocating church life.

From 1960 to 1964, Georgi Vins was actively involved in a series of meetings and writing of documents to the state authorities, to the All-Union Council, and to believers throughout the Soviet

Union. Finally, the Reform Baptists officially went into schism on September 18-19, 1965 at a secret meeting in Moscow when they adopted the name Council of Evangelical Christian-Baptist Churches. The history of this period began to be constructed in the West only in the middle of the 1960s when documents found their way out of the Soviet Union, and the earliest, which indicates Vins' involvement, is dated October 21, 1964. It is titled "Address to all Servants of the Evangelical Christian-Baptist Church" and consists of forty-one pages of applied theological reasoning on the theme of sanctification in which Vins and the six other signatories set forth and justify the position they have taken up.

The Reform Baptists persistently requested the government to be permitted to hold a congress and to be freed from persecution for their faith. Their requests were not met, and on May 16-17, 1966, they took the bold step of holding a public demonstration in Moscow in support of their claims. On May 19th, Vins and the other chief Reform Baptist leader, Gennadi Kryuchkov, walked openly into the offices of the building of the Central Committee of the Communist Party as representatives of the suppressed demonstrators. Both were arrested and held with about thirty other demonstrators in Lefortovo Prison. Information about them was not forthcoming for some time. An article on the Baptists in a major Soviet newspaper, *Sovietskaya Rossiya*, dated November 22, 1966 gave the impression that both Vins and Kryuchkov were at liberty.

It was at this very time, however, that the trial was taking place—November 29-30, 1966 in a Moscow court. Almost no believers were admitted, and the audience was markedly hostile. Vins and Kryuchkov were both extremely tired after two grueling days of trial with almost no breaks for rests or meals. An adjournment was refused, however, and they had to make their final speeches despite their exhaustion. The first day of the trial lasted from 10 a.m. to 9 p.m. and the second day from 10 a.m. to 2 a.m. A full transcript of the trial has been published in *Faith on Trial in Russia*.

Both defendants were sentenced to three years' imprisonment under article 142/2 of the Criminal Code.

Letters from the Council of Prisoners' Relatives written during 1968 said that Vins had been sent to a prison in Perm region in February 1967. It gave his home address in Kiev, where his family still live at the present time. In the summer of 1967, he was transferred to Kizel prison, also in Perm region. Vins' own diary describes his journey through the labor camps, and the results of his Christian witness there.

The Council of Prisoners' Relatives reported that by February 1968, his physical condition had seriously deteriorated. He had contracted an infection which led to heart disease, and he had

Lefortovo Prison

running sores on his arms and body. Despite this, and the fact that he was trained as an electrical engineer, he was forced to drag logs at work. The "Open Letter" to Brezhnev, Kosygin, Podgorny and others dated February 25, 1968, which contains this information, goes on to say that threats had been made to liquidate him, that his Bible had been taken away, that he had been forced to renounce visits from his family, and that some of the parcels sent to him had been returned. However, Vins' diary records an unexpected meeting with his mother and elder daughter on March 30th, 1968, his mother's birthday.

Three months later, in a statement dated May 15th, 1968, the Council of Prisoners' Relatives reported that, though healthy when sentenced, he now suffered from high blood pressure, heart disease, and a double inguinal hernia threatened with strangulation. Vins himself records that his health worsened abruptly in January 1968.*

His diary refers only in passing to his physical condition, however. Mostly, his thoughts, and the sixteen poems in which some of them are expressed, are concerned with his reflections on his surroundings, thoughts of his loved ones, and meditations on his faith. The three poles of his existence revealed in his diary are Christ, his mother, and Russia.

Vins was released in May of 1969, having refused the offer of an early release held out by the KGB in return for his cooperation with them against the church. His state of health was such that he had to undergo two operations after his release.

Meanwhile, his family had also suffered because of his prisoner status. His wife, despite the fact she has a university degree in foreign languages, had to take a job selling ice cream His daughter Natasha, according to the Open Letter of May 25th, 1968, was "terrorized at school."

---

*Georgi was 39 years old at this time.

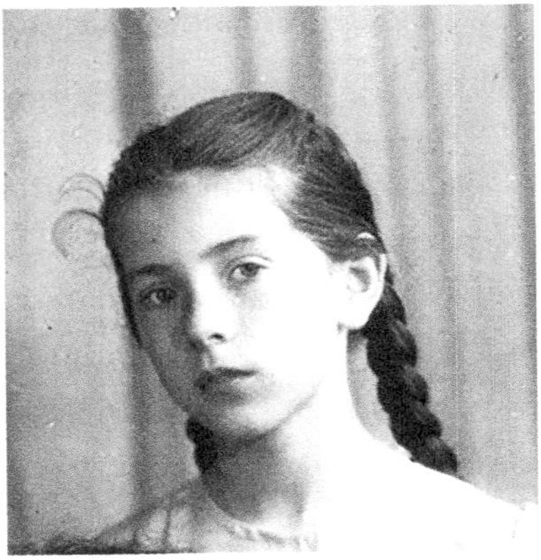

Natasha Vins - 10 years old

This brings us to the end of the time covered by Vins' autobiographical account in the "Family Chronicle," but it is far from being the end of his suffering for his Christian faith. The documents of the Council of Prisoners' Relatives continue the story.

By the end of 1969, Vins (now 40 years old) was once more taking an active part in the life of the Council of Churches. The All-Union Council invited him to attend their December congress, but he refused this invitation. The Council of Churches Congress held on December 6th in Tula took this decision collectively. The congress elected Georgi Vins Secretary of the Council of Churches (with Gennadi Kryuchkov as Chairman).

It was not long, however, before Vins' activity as a pastor was curtailed once more. His election as an officer of the Kiev community should have guaranteed immunity from the obligation to do secular work. However, petty restrictions and interference continued.

Georgi Vins, 1964

The Procuracy summoned Vins in 1969 in connection with a sermon he had recently preached. On January 21st, 1970, the authorities imposed a minor sentence—one year of "forced labor." This entails compulsory work, with "clocking in," and a deduction of wages, but the person concerned is able to continue living at home. They assigned Vins to a Kiev factory.

By June or July 1970, a new criminal case against Vins was in preparation. The context was the renewed persecution of the Kiev community, which had applied to register a church according to the correct procedure but had been refused. On August 17th, Vins received a summons to appear at 9 a.m. on August 31st at the procuracy of Dnepropetrevsk district, Kiev, bringing his passport with him. (All Soviet citizens carry an internal passport or identity card.) He was summoned under suspicion as a criminal under article 209/2 of the Criminal Code. A second (undated) summons for August 28th was issued when Vins failed to obey the first.

A letter from Vins to the Procurator dated August 28th explains why he did not obey either summons. He complains of persecution, despite the fact he is an elected officer of the church. Persecution is continuing at work and the two new summons demonstrate that a new criminal case against him is in preparation. Therefore, he has decided to leave the factory in order to continue his spiritual ministry full time.

Vins had to leave his home and family to fulfill his church duties. With the police looking for him, he had to stay on the run. We do not know how he lived, but we must presume there were believers who gave him food and shelter. It was probably during this period in hiding that Vins wrote "A Family Chronicle" and "Faithful Servants of God."

The Council of Prisoners' Relatives' "Urgent Communication" of October 1st, 1970 said that Vins had been tried in his absence on September 29th and sentenced to be taken into custody for investigation as a parasite. (In the Soviet Union, a person without work is liable to be declared a "parasite," a serious crime.) This meant there were two cases against him in two Kiev procuracies. His home had been searched for religious literature, and the militia was harassing his family and searching the homes of other members of the church.

For over three years, Georgi Vins lived in hiding, unable to return home, and attempting to carry on his work as a pastor clandestinely. He was apparently not arrested or imprisoned during this time. He was certainly free on December 10th, 1970 to write a letter from his home address in Kiev to Kosygin, Brezhnev, Podgerny ,and Rudenko (the Procurator General of the USSR) in protest of his mother's arrest.

Lydia Vins was arrested on December 1st, 1970 (she was 63 at the time). The Council of Prisoners' Relatives reports that the police came to her home, where her sudden arrest caused great distress to her grandchildren, who were in her care during the absence of her daughter-in-law. The Council considers that her arrest was a direct result of her activity as president of the Council of Prisoners' Relatives in compiling and distributing information about Christian prisoners. They appealed for her in a letter to U Thant dated December 12th, 1970, signed, among others, by Georgi's wife, Nadezhda.

Georgi Vins' letter to the Soviet leaders shows special concern over his mother's extremely poor health. The militiamen carrying out her arrest were forced to send for a doctor to accompany her to the prison. She was held in Lukyanov prison in Kiev.

The Christian activity of Georgi and Lydia Vins provoked the Soviet atheist establishment to write a critical article about the family in the December 1970 issue of *Man and the World*, the Ukrainian monthly atheist journal.

The tone of the article is hostile, but some of the details it contains may be accurate. It is the only source for the following biographical information. It says that Peter Vins married Lydia Zharikova in Omsk, after which they moved to Novosibirsk. Georgi went to School No. 30 in Omsk, then to an electro-mechanical technical institute, then to a Kiev polytechnic. His fellow students apparently say he used to receive full marks for classes in Marxism-Leninism and political economy. Georgi's wife Nadezhda Ivanovna graduated in Romance and German languages from Kiev University. His mother Lydia, the article states, is a bookkeeper by profession. It goes on to add in a hostile tone that she has in fact been married three times, and

A 1962 photo of Lydia Vins

it calls her Lydia Zharikova-Vins-Vlasova-Shuldeshova. One should note that there is nowhere any record of other marriages*; Lydia is still living with Georgi's family and signs herself Lydia Vins. The article says it was in 1963 that Georgi Vins gave up his job in a design institute and became an itinerant pastor.

The Kiev church came to the defense of the Vins family in a statement dated January 6th, 1971, which was signed by 180 believers. They protested against slanders in the *Man and the World* article, the persecution of Georgi, and the arrest of Lydia, for whom they requested release on the ground of her illness.

An "Open Letter" of April 10th, 1971 reports that Lydia Vins was tried in Kiev on February 8th-9th. (The "Family Chronicle" gives the text of her defense speech.) Georgi Vins' wife, elder daughter, and son were present, together with about fifteen Christians, although about a hundred had wanted to attend. Lydia appealed without success on February 18th. She was sentenced to three years imprisonment. The Council of Prisoners' Relatives Bulletin, No. 2, 1971 gave the text of her defense speech and a review of her case. A prisoner list issued in April 1971 gave her camp address in Kharkov, and Bulletin, No. 3 gives further details about her poor health; she is diabetic, has a stomach illness, and has to be physically supported on the way to work.

She was later moved to another camp, in Dnepropetrovsk, according to a prisoner list dated January 1972. The Council of

*This is verifiably untrue about Lydia Vins, who was married only to Peter Vins.

Prisoners' Relatives expressed grave concern that she might not survive her three-year sentence because of her illness, but later stated that she had been moved to a civil hospital for a month, after which she was taken back to the labor camp. Her health was still very bad, however, and the Kiev congregation once more appealed for her release.

A report reaching the West in April 1974 said Lydia Vins had been released in November 1973; she was very weak and was staying with friends in the Ukraine.

Apparently, Georgi Vins was still in hiding. He is mentioned in an officially published Soviet booklet, *Legislation on Religious Cults*, by A. Sedyulin, published in 1974, which criticizes him in a brief paragraph for refusing to "follow a way of life worthy of a Soviet man." According to Sedyulin "he is now in hiding both from justice and from his family."

On March 30th, 1974, Georgi Vins was arrested again. He was held incommunicado for the next six months. On April 15th, the Kiev congregation appealed for his release to Soviet leaders. On April 18th, the four Vins children—Natasha, Petya, Liza, and Zhenya—also addressed a letter to the Soviet leaders (see Appendix). They are anxious about their father's poor health and fear that he will die and be posthumously rehabilitated like their grandfather. They recount the persecution their family has undergone: the prison sentences of both their grandparents, their mother's inability to find work in the field for which she is qualified, and now recent measures against the children themselves. The eldest, Natasha, was dismissed on January 9th, 1974 from her job at a Kiev hospital by a doctor who told her that religion and medicine were incompatible.* Petya, who has just left school, has been unable to find work anywhere.

The Kiev congregation addressed themselves once more to the Soviet leaders in a statement of April 21st, signed by 174 members

---

*Natasha's autobiography, *Children of the Storm*, chronicles her childhood in the Soviet Union.

of the church. They assert that Vins was arrested on charges of vagrancy and that such charges are unfounded. They beg, among other things, for the release of Vins and all Baptist prisoners. An appeal by them of the same date is addressed to all believers in the USSR, asking them to pray for Vins' health and his release from prison. They say he is being held in a Kiev prison.

Vins' family appealed to the Soviet leaders in two telegrams dated April 25th. The first, from Vins' wife, mother, and children, requested an interview with him to ascertain his condition as he had by then been in prison for nearly a month without specific charges. The second, from Lydia Vins alone, denies the assertion of a Kiev official for religious affairs that her son is a state criminal and says that if he is not released, she will inform all believers and international organizations. This telegram includes the information that Vins is being held in Lukyanov prison in Kiev.

A telegram from Nadezhda Vins states that the family had requested a meeting with Vins after clothes which they had sent to him on May 13th were returned to them, leading them to suppose that he was either dead or seriously ill in hospital.

A message from Lydia Vins in August 1974 said that she was disappointed at the lack of action and publicity in the West to support her son. She asked that an attempt be made to get a Christian doctor or doctors from the West to give him a medical examination. She said the family went to the Kiev procuracy on May 16th hoping for a meeting with Vins, but this was refused. Officials handled them roughly and threw one of them down the stairs.

An undated declaration of support for Vins, demanding his release, has been sent to Soviet leaders from believers in widely scattered places, including Kharkov, Zaporozhe, Dnepropetrovsk, Crimea, and Kirovograd regions. They say they have seen short reports in the press that he was arrested for vagrancy.

Another appeal on behalf of Georgi Vins indicates that the Baptists have some contact with the Moscow human rights movement. Academician Sakharov, founder of the unofficial Human Rights Committee in Moscow, in an appeal to the World Council of Churches dated September 11th, 1974, asked them to intercede for Vins (see Appendix). He refers also to the persecution suffered by many Baptists and those of other faiths. Sakharov's appeal included the news that Vins had been on a hunger strike for four months and that his trial was expected soon.

Lydia Vins appealed again for her son on September 29th, asking for help as his trial was imminent (see Appendix). She gives details of the charges brought against him, under which he could be deprived of freedom for ten years. Her appeals were directed abroad. One was to Amnesty International, which responded, saying the organization was ready to send an observer to the trial.

Academician Sakharov issued a second appeal for Georgi Vins on October 22nd (see Appendix). This time it was signed by three colleagues on the Human Rights Committee and was addressed to the World Council of Churches and Amnesty International. Their letter takes up the point raised by Lydia Vins' letter, that article 209 of the Ukrainian Criminal Code, under which Georgi Vins is to be tried, is being used more and more often against Baptists. Under this, they can be given a ten-year sentence, more than under other articles, which indicates that the authorities are taking an increasingly hard line with them. The appeal vigorously defends Vins against the charge of "living on the means of believers, and, in this way, infringing their material rights," under which he is to be tried. It concludes with a defense of all believers whose rights are violated by the state.

The appeals by Sakharov are significant: this is the first time that the Human Rights Committee has made a separate statement in defense of a Baptist. This creates a link between the Baptists, who were the first to organize regular appeals for human rights in the Soviet Union, and the Human Rights Committee, which in recent years has gained worldwide prestige.

In December in Moscow, officials of the Baptist World Alliance made personal pleas on Vins' behalf and various American Senators added their voices. Senator Harold Hughes wrote to Dr. Henry Kissinger, asking him to look into the facts of the case and to make the strongest possible protests on behalf of the American people.

Positive efforts were made to comply with Mrs. Lydia Vins' request that her son be defended at his trial by a Christian lawyer from the West. On November 26th, the "Mission to Iron Curtain Countries" (Misjon bak Jernteppet) in Norway wrote an urgent letter to the International Commission of Jurists in Geneva.

> Recently we received a letter from the USSR with an urgent appeal to seek juridical assistance on the occasion of the trial of the arrested church leader, Georgi Vins. The letter is signed by Vins' mother, his wife, and two children . . .
>
> We urgently request that the International Commission of Jurists take the necessary steps to meet the request for help from a Christian lawyer in the West. If such an assistance is in contradiction to Soviet law, we request that you do your utmost to secure a lawyer from the West to be present at the trial with the status of official observer.
>
> If, owing to financial difficulties, you should not be able to comply with the request, the Norwegian "Mission to Iron Curtain Countries" is willing to pay all the costs involved with fees and transport.
>
> We should also like to inform you that we have consulted a Norwegian Russian-speaking lawyer with the appropriate qualifications. Provided you find it a satisfactory arrangement, he might be willing to undertake the mission as your representative.

The International Commission of Jurists responded by authorizing two men to act as its representatives.

In December, a group of Norwegian parliamentarians applied for visas to attend the trial. They were Mrs. Bergfrid Fjose, Mrs. Sigfrid Utkilen, and Mr. Ragnar Udjus. The group was to have been accompanied by the painter Victor Sparre, Judge Alf Lind Haerem, and an interpreter, Mr. Guibrand Overbye. The last two were also to act as representatives of the International Commission of Jurists. However, the applications for visas were returned from the Soviet Embassy without any comment whatsoever.

In London, when the Soviet Ambassador and his guests recently celebrated the 57th anniversary of the Soviet Revolution, they were confronted by young people with banners appealing for Vins.

Despite this Western support, Vins' trial began at a Kiev court (15 Vladimirskaya St.) on January 27th, 1975 and continued for five days. His mother has since written an account of it dated February 24th, 1975. Though it was kept secret from the Vins family and other believers, Lydia Vins writes, "the Lord enabled us to learn of the day of the trial." Only with great difficulty could the family penetrate the strong army guard and enter the courtroom. Other believers waited outside in the frost and cold for the five days of the trial.

At the beginning of the trial, Vins rejected the lawyer the court provided, "an atheist state official" in Lydia Vins' words. He had asked for a Christian lawyer from abroad "since we do not have any such in this country." Alf Haerem from Norway was willing to take the case, but he was denied an entry visa to the USSR. Vins refused to recognize the court on two grounds: "1) It is a one-sided atheist court. It is not I who am on trial, but the whole Evangelical Christian-Baptist faith. The Bible, the Gospel, our whole movement is on trial. 2) The investigation has taken place with extreme violence, with the use of physical and mental terror. The investigation has been conducted not by state lawyers but by the KGB." Vins actually identified a KGB officer who he said had threatened him over a period of two months: "[T]here he is in the fourth row, on the fourth chair at the end, and his name is . . ."

Vins then submitted eighteen requests to the court regarding the conduct of the trial, but none of them were met. Lydia Vins alleges that cross-examination of the witnesses was biased and says that none of the witnesses requested by her son were called. When Vins was asked for his opinion, he refused to answer, saying that his defense lawyer Alf Haerem should have answered. He did explain, however, that he believed a campaign to annihilate Christianity was being waged in the USSR and backed this up with statistics. He said he could have been at home by now had he agreed to KGB invitations to collaborate with them within the Council of Churches.

Experts investigating the case then spoke, though the whole of their findings was not read out. One of the charges, "falsifying Soviet reality," was based on the essays translated in this book, the "Family Chronicle" and "Faithfulness" (here titled "Faithful Servants of God") which allegedly "was directed against the state, was criminal and contained lies."

When Georgi Vins was given an opportunity to defend himself, he merely said, "My defense should be conducted by Alf Haerem. But now I leave my whole case with my Lord Jesus Christ." The sentence proposed was five years' labor camp and five years' exile in Siberia, with confiscation of property.

Lydia Vins continues:

> The sentence was announced the next day. When it was read out to him and they asked: "Have you understood?"—he said: "Yes. Glory to Jesus Christ."
>
> Then Christians gave his relatives flowers—roses, carnations, narcissi. Until then, the flowers had been concealed under their clothes. These flowers were thrown to him. Georgi's son took them and threw them saying: "Daddy, these are for

you and your bravery." His wife threw flowers to him saying, "You have won this trial." Also his daughter. The whole room clapped. When the flowers were thrown, everyone fell silent. The whole room was full of people with invitation cards.

They applauded and laughed. His daughter Natasha climbed on a seat and said, "No, daddy, the church will not die (a reference to one of his poems) just as the love of Christ does not die. With Christ you are free in prison. And freedom without Him is prison."

Usually he was led out last, but this time first. He went out carrying the flowers and saying, "Greetings to all friends." By this time, there were more than 500 believers outside the building and about 200 who had come by bus and tram. They were all waiting for this moment and holding bouquets of flowers. But he was secretly led out another way. Then all the believers removed their headgear and began to sing. It was very moving. The group of 500 sang—everybody sang. Everything was still, no one moved. Then I came out with my grandson, leaning on his arm. He took off his cap, as at a funeral. They opened up to let us through, and we made our way home. But the day before all the young people had gone through the back entrance to the place where his prison car stood. And he heard them singing the song, "For the faith of the Gospel . . ." Police came up, but nothing could be done until he was taken away. This was the trial.

Four days later, a family meeting was permitted, although only Georgi's wife and son and the three small children were permitted to see him: his mother and eldest daughter were not admitted. A glass door or wall was between them and the conversation, which was certainly monitored, was conducted through telephone booths. Vins was reluctant to appeal against his sentence, but his family begged him to do so, though they were not told subsequently whether he had or not. He asked for very warm clothing so he had probably been told he would be sent to deepest Siberia.

Lydia Vins' report of the trial is remarkable for its courage, optimism, and faith. In particular, she thanks God for the prayers of Christians the world over which helped her son. "When I saw him during the trial, tormented and pale, with sunken eyes, I thought: *he hasn't slept for nights.* The trial lasted five days. But when we parted, he said, 'I was able to go to sleep peacefully every night. It was a very great mercy of God. It is surely due to the many prayers of God's children.'" Lydia Vins says that she herself has had the same experience in prison, and so have many others. "Many who have been in prison have testified that they felt people's prayers, and they knew not simply those days when they were prayed for, but the actual hours. This is the testimony of more than one prisoner. It was the same with me, too. And it was the same with my son who said at the trial, 'I felt the prayers of God's children and these prayers gave me strength and brought me back to life.' We are wholeheartedly grateful first to the Lord for His faithfulness and also to the Christians of the whole world for their prayers."

Georgi Vins, in prison in 1977

We cannot know what is happening to Georgi Vins now in prison, but we can get a glimpse of it from the diary he wrote when last imprisoned, which forms the central part of the "Family Chronicle." Behind the events we have described lies a family man who loves his country deeply. He has proved himself to be a great Christian leader. Here he speaks to us in his own words.

Jane Ellis
Keston College, March 1975

I am convinced that faith is strengthened by trial, and that God offers spiritual comfort in proportion to one's physical suffering. The imprisoned Christian derives support from God and prayer, which are sources of never-ending strength.[1]—**Georgi P. Vins**

Part I: A Family Chronicle

BY GEORGI VINS

To My Persecutors

My persecutors, I do not curse you,
And at this hour under the burden of the cross
I pray for you and bless you
With the simple humanity of Christ.

I am pure before you: by word and deeds
I have called you to good and to light.
I have so much wished that your hearts
Would be possessed by the lofty ideal of Love.

But rejecting this kind summons
You answered with rabid enmity.
My persecutors, I do not curse you,
But I am saddened by your fate.

The immortal examples of history
Speak of the futility of persecution—
The fires of love and abundant faith
Burn enthusiastically through the whole land!

My persecutors, I do not curse you,
And at this hour under the burden of the cross
I pray for you and bless you
With the simple humanity of Christ.

December 1968
"Anyusha" Corrective Labor Camp

INTRODUCTION

This is an ordinary chronicle of a normal Christian family, one of the many thousands in our country. Persecution, prison, and exile for their faith have become a traditional way of life for the Christians of Russia.

These pages set forth memories of my father, Peter Yakovlevich Vins, a preacher of the Gospel in the 1930s in Siberia and the Far East, who was physically annihilated in 1943 in one of the labor camps of Magadan.

In the section "My Labor Camp Diary" are set forth in chronological sequence, with commentaries, some poems I wrote during my imprisonment from 1966-1969.

I also quote letters from my mother, which I received in the camps of Perm region, and which the Lord has helped me to preserve until now despite numerous searches both in the camps and at "liberty."

Some facts about the arrest and trial of my mother in 1970 and 1971 are also cited.

Peter J. Vins and young Georgi

MEMORIES OF MY FATHER, PETER J. VINS

FIRST ARREST

> By faith Moses, when he was come to years, refused to be called the son of Pharaoh's daughter; Choosing rather to suffer affliction with the people of God, than to enjoy the pleasures of sin for a season; Esteeming the reproach of Christ greater riches than the treasures in Egypt: for he had respect unto the recompence of the reward. (Hebrews 11: 24-26)

Every time I read Hebrews chapter 11, verses 14 to 26, I involuntarily recall that these were my father's favorite verses. Like many Russian Christians of his time, he had a profound understanding of the biblical truth that it is better to suffer with God's people and better to bear the vilification of Christ than to have transient sinful enjoyment and earthly treasures.

There are no greater riches than Christ, and you feel this especially keenly when they want to take Him away from you, when they forbid you to share these riches with people. But people need Him so much!

Jesus—is there any name more dear to a redeemed soul?

You are near to me, as the shore is to the sea,
You are dear to me, as water is to earth,
You came to make grief sweet
And to light the fire of love in the shadows.

Without you, I do not need life,
Without you, I merely breathe.
You alone are the joy of my soul.
Be always with me, I beg you!

Thus wrote a Christian poet.

How fortunate those children are those who have a loving father and mother beside them!

It is a great blessing if the parents who have given their children life have given them not only a good upbringing, education, and a vocation but also their own Christian life, if, in short, they have pointed to Christ—a man's best friend! What good fortune it is to have parents who are one's own, not only in the flesh but, in spirit and in faith!

And if the parents were found worthy to suffer for Christ and even, fettered, to drink to the dregs the cup of death, then for their son or daughter their feat of faith becomes a sacred example of lofty self-sacrificing Christian love and calls them to be faithful to the Lord.

The first time my father was arrested was in Moscow in 1930 [when he was 32], and I was two years old. At that time, he was participating in the work of the Assembly of the Union of Evangelical Christians-Baptists as the representative of the brotherhood of Evangelical Christians-Baptists of the Far East. On his arrival in Moscow, my father was summoned to the

NKVD* where it was suggested to him that at the Assembly he should support the candidatures of the ministers B. and K., who had been selected by the government bodies as members of the administrative board of the Baptist Union. My father was very surprised by the authorities' suggestion, which was manifest interference in the internal life of the church and refused to support these candidatures. Within a few days, he was arrested. As for B. and K., they were elected just the same to the administrative board of the Baptist Union. B. revealed himself as a traitor not long afterwards when the President of the Baptist Union, Nikolai Vasilievich Odintsov, was arrested. In 1935, B. contributed a good deal to the actual closing of the Baptist Union.[2]

Beginning in the 1930s, pressure on prominent workers in religious societies was intensified, and apostates were advanced to positions of leadership with the aim of corrupting the church from the inside. My father spent three months under investigation in Butyrki prison and was then sentenced to three years in labor camp. At that time in Blagoveshchensk-on-Amur, his son, who had just begun to talk, would kneel down with his mother and repeat just four words: "Jesus! Bring Daddy back!"

During those years, Father passed under guard through many prisoners' convoys, prisons, and labor camps in the Far East and the Northern Urals. In the Far East, he was taken in convoy to a labor camp situated on the shore of Svetlaya Bay.

One day in a town in the Far East, a column of prisoners was being marched from a transit prison to a goods station for embarkation. After the column ran, weeping women, seeing off their fathers, husbands, sons . . . A young Orthodox priest was marching in the column beside my father. His wife was hurrying alongside after the column. As she took leave of him, she cried, "Vasya! Don't lose heart! The darker the night, the brighter are the stars!" The

---

* NKVD: "People's Commissariat for Internal Affairs." The name of the Soviet secret police from 1934 to 1946.

priest's heartening reply rang out above the column of prisoners, "The deeper the sorrow, the nearer is God!"

About ten Orthodox priests were serving their sentences in the labor camp at Svetlaya Bay, and they worked as orderlies in the prison hospital. They behaved very warmly and sympathetically to my father and even got him a job as an orderly in the hospital. In 1932, my father sent me a poem from this camp for my birthday. I have kept it carefully. It is very dear to me because it contains the sacred testament of a prisoner-father to his four-year-old son. Here are some lines from this poem:

Now you are forced involuntarily
To suffer for the name of the Lord,
But I pray that you may willingly
Choose the thorny path of Christ.

When the golden days of childhood
Have passed by, and, as a young man,
You turn your clear eyes
Into the lands of your dreams,

Then give up all your strength of will,
All the dreams of your heart,
Your unpolluted life and destiny—
Everything to His service!

For a Christian, there is always a Svetlaya* Bay in Christ Jesus! Neither the storms of persecution nor the darkness of unbelief are able to take away his bright hope in Christ!

For some time, Father was in camps in the Northern Urals. He was taken in a train load of convicts to Usolye (now Solikamsk)

*Literal meaning: "bright."

and then marched in convoy another 300 kilometers to the north, to one of the timber-felling camps of the *taiga*.*

In 1967, I also visited these places, also under guard. Like my father, I was taken in convoy to Solikamsk and then not on foot but in open lorries under the guard of soldiers and watchdogs 200 kilometers further north.

As we drove along the old convoy roads, I remembered my father. Perhaps in the '30s, he had walked along these very same roads.

The valleys and hill of the Urals,
The green sea of forests.
Here your path lay,
Here your love died away!

You walked through storms and tempests,
And heard the howl of wild beasts,
But early in spring the birch trees
Were whispering: "Stand firm, my son!"

I wrote these lines in 1967 in one of the Urals labor camps, recalling the chains of my father.

AT LIBERTY

In the summer of 1933, father was released. Mother and I traveled to Novosibirsk to meet him. Here he was faced with the journey to Biisk, which at that time was a small town lost among the forests of the Altai.

Father did not receive a passport when he was released but was directed to a place of residence in Biisk with the status of an exile. We

*Taiga—coniferous forest in the north of the Soviet Union, but to the south of the bleak tundra region of the Arctic.

traveled in a passenger train. I can still remember the overcrowded carriage, the shouting, and the swearing. Somehow, I was settled in the upper berth where I could go to sleep, and my parents slept sitting up. At the station in Biisk, we were robbed, reducing our belongings, which were meager enough anyway.

We settled down somewhere on the outskirts of the town, taking a room in a private house. It was a very beautiful spot. Around us was a pine forest and silence. In the winter, Father and I would take a sledge and wander through the forest. I dearly loved these walks.

There were believers in Biisk, but the prayer house was closed, and they used to gather in houses.

My parents were extremely poor. A conviction for religious beliefs and the absence of a passport were a great obstacle to arranging employment. Many places refused to enroll Father for work. Finally, my father and mother found work, but a long way from home—across the river on the opposite side of town. In the autumn slush and the winter frosts and snowstorms, it took them two or three hours very often on foot to reach their place of work.

My parents were often ill . . . I remember that first my father would lie in bed with a high temperature, and my mother would bustle round him and tend him, and then she herself would be ill and Father would be the doctor.

One day, Father received a letter from Blagoveshchensk, from his home community, where he had served as pastor from 1926 to 1930 until the day of his arrest. This kind message with its words of brotherly love encouraged and comforted Father in this most difficult period of his wandering. The Lord preserved this letter amidst numerous searches in the following decades. Through His faithful children, the Lord also sent daily bread in this critical period of our lives.

In January 1934, Father received a passport and permission to leave his place of exile. We moved to Novosibirsk. The meeting place there had not yet been closed. I remember how Father used to take me with him to the prayer house, which was situated on the outskirts of the town. It was very exciting for me to walk along the streets with my father. It seemed as though everyone was looking at me: see, I have a father too! I loved to sit beside him at the meeting and sing together about Jesus, who had heard my prayers and brought my daddy back!

The same year my grandmother, Mariya Abramovna Zharikova, a true and virtuous Christian, came to Novosibirsk. She stayed there for a while and then went off to Blagoveshchensk taking me with her for a while.

I met my parents again in 1935 in Omsk where they had moved. At that time, the prayer house in the town had already been taken away. The believers had built it on the bank of the River Om. Now mounted militia had been quartered there. The believers began to meet in a small private house on the outskirts of the town behind the station. In those years, there were still no trams in Omsk, and it was a very long and difficult journey to reach the meeting.

My father used to visit meetings of believers and continued to witness about Christ. Furthermore, he visited believers at home; he encouraged, comforted, and strengthened those who had weakened spiritually. With him went his friend Anton Pavlovich Martynenko, an evangelist of the Far East Union of Christians-Baptists, the father of a large family, who had already suffered exile in the Far East for the Word of God and had found a temporary haven in Omsk. Anton Pavlovich was tall, with an open, courageous face; he was a most wonderful Christian, always joyful, never downhearted, a true servant of the Lord.

During the day, they worked, my father in the administrative office of the town pharmacy and Anton Pavlovich as a carpenter on one of the construction sites, and they devoted every evening to the encouragement and comfort of the believers in that difficult time for the church. In 1935, a prominent worker in the Far East Baptist Union, V.P., arrived in Omsk with his family. He did not join in the believers' meetings but stayed at home and tried to spread his mood of depression among others. My father and Anton Pavlovich had to talk a great deal with him, trying to encourage V.P. and lessen the influence on others of his spirit of fear and timeserving. But V.P. never fulfilled his role as a minister.

FATHER'S SERMONS

I have preserved rough copies of my father's sermons and his summaries and letters to believers written in Omsk in 1935. I include below one of his sermons (in abridged form) and one of his letters to believers.

"The Completion of What is Lacking in Christ's Afflictions" (by Peter Vins)

> Who now rejoice in my sufferings for you, and fill up that which is behind of the afflictions of Christ in my flesh for his body's sake, which is the church. (Colossians 1:24)

At a superficial reading, the words of our text give rise to a certain perplexity, and the question arises: surely Christ's sacrifice is sufficient for our salvation? Surely the apostle Paul's sufferings were not necessary for the fulfillment of what is lacking?

Let us look more closely at these questions. Scripture says clearly that the sacrifice of Christ is entirely sufficient for our salvation:

> Who his own self bare our sins in his own body on the tree. (1 Peter 2:24)

"It is finished" (John 19:30). These words uttered by the Lord on the cross are an undeniable proof of the sufficiency of this suffering for our salvation (see Hebrews 10:10-14). Paul says that by his sufferings he supplies "that which is behind [lacking] in the afflictions of Christ . . . for . . . the church."

There are two ideas here which must be mastered.

The *first* idea is that there is *insufficient recognition* of the afflictions of Christ: of the afflictions which the Lord underwent as He walked with His firm, courageous, sure step overcoming the sufferings of Gethsemane and Golgotha, the humiliation, the shame, and the loneliness.

This lack (in recognition) Paul completed when he endured what is described in 1 Corinthians 4:9-13; 2 Corinthians 4:8-18; and 2 Corinthians 6:3-10.

Therefore, Paul did not shun sufferings and hardship, realizing that just as he and other apostles claimed their strength from the matchless conduct of the Lord, foreseeing and enduring suffering, so the believers must and would be encouraged by his chains and his privations (Philippians 1:14).

The *second* idea is that Paul suffered not for his faults, not as a thief or a murderer. He suffered "for . . . the church." He suffered for Christ's Gospel. He bore everything "for the elect's sakes, that they may also obtain the salvation which is in Christ Jesus" (2 Timothy 2:10; see also 2 Timothy 1:8, 12, and 2:8-9).

But is it conceivable that Paul alone compensated for this lack? No! By his words, "us the apostles last" (1 Corinthians 4:9; and see 2 Corinthians 6:1), Paul joins others also to this service of the completion of what is lacking in Christ's afflictions.

To this number undoubtedly belong Stephen, the first martyr, who was stoned to death, James, the brother of John, who was beheaded by Herod, Peter, who was beaten before the Sanhedrin, John, who was exiled to the island of Patmos, and Timothy, who suffered imprisonment (Hebrews 13:23).

To this number should be added Polycarp, the Bishop of the church of Smyrna who lived in the second century, Jan Hus, who was burnt at the stake in the fourteenth century, John Bunyan, who spent fourteen years in a damp dungeon, and millions of others (according to the calculations of some), who proved their love and devotion to Christ, dying in the Roman amphitheaters at the hands of gladiators and wild beasts of prey crazed with hunger, and from torments in the torture chambers, and on the fires of the Inquisition, branded as foes, traitors, and heretics.

To this glorious company of the saints, of whom the whole world was not worthy, our brothers and sisters suffering for Christ today also belong. God has had such chosen people in every generation. He has them in our time also.

But is it worth enumerating their names on paper, when their names are inscribed in God's memory and in the memory of His faithful people? For were His servants ever such a spectacle as they are in our time?

How then must we, members of His body, behave to those who are suffering in this way for His church?

First, we must pray for them. If Paul, the apostle to the Gentiles, stood in need of the prayer of others for himself, and begged for it, how much more do our brothers and sisters on whose shoulders lies this heavy burden of suffering? Pray that they may always feel the blessing promised by God (Matthew 5:10-12), that they may not lose heart, but that on the contrary they may be an example to us all by their steadfastness and courage.

Secondly, we must lighten their sufferings, taking on to ourselves part of the burden of worry about their families, and at times about themselves.

A New Year's Letter from Father
December 12th, 1935

Yet another year has come to its end. A year which seems to have begun only yesterday. A year which has brought to many of the Lord's faithful no little grief, suffering, and hardship. A year when more than one tear was shed.

A year when the Lord like an eagle destroyed through circumstances more than one nest of cherished hopes, dreams, and private plans, but then caught us up and bore us on His wings to teach us to walk by faith and not by sight, that is, by senses or feelings (Deuteronomy 32:11-12; 2 Corinthians 5:7).

We are called to live by faith (Romans 1:17; Colossians 2:6). By faith, we accepted Jesus as our Savior from judgment and the damnation due to sin.

By faith, we claim the wonderful "power of his resurrection" (Philippians 3:10), the power which every day and every hour by the death of Christ on the cross frees us who "being dead to sins" (1 Peter 2:24) and who always bear "in the body the dying [the death] of the Lord Jesus" (2 Corinthians 4:10), from the dominion and supremacy of sin in our flesh.

By faith, we strengthen our sometimes-trembling hearts with the thought that He who has promised is faithful to deliver us in His own time and hour from the presence and nearness of sin by taking us to Himself.

But surely He who showed such care for our souls, and has gone on showing it until now, will not be indifferent to the fate and the needs of our bodies? Having given His life for the deliverance of our souls, will He grudge the food and clothing necessary for our bodies? The Savior Himself answers this question in the words recorded in the Gospel of Matthew 6:25-34.

In the past year, as in previous years, we have once again experienced God's marvelous care and faithfulness toward our spirits, souls, and bodies. There is no doubt that God, who invites us to cast "all your care upon him" (1 Peter 5:7) and promises to care for us, will fulfil this in the coming year also. So let us cast all our anxieties on Him, whether they be about work, food, clothing, or safety, for God says:

And even to your old age I am he; and even to hoar [grey] hairs will I carry you: I have made, and I will bear; even I will carry, and will deliver you. (Isaiah 46:4)

May the conclusion of the psalmist be ours also, "For this God is our God for ever and ever: he will be our guide even unto death" (Psalm 48: 14).

I sincerely greet all who are faithful to the Lord and wish them a joyful day of remembrance of the birth of our Lord in Bethlehem, and also a happy New Year.

Yours in the Lord,
P. Vins.

SECOND ARREST

In Omsk, we lived on the outskirts of the town. My parents took a room in a large wooden house belonging to an unbeliever.

One evening, there was an unfamiliar knock on the door. The owner asked, "Who is it?"

The answer came, "Police, open up!" It was NKVD agents. They asked for Father and produced a warrant for his arrest.

The officer in charge of the arrest and the search looked around the modest furnishings of the room: an old wooden bed, a table, a large wooden chest which served as a wardrobe, and a divan, which at night was my bed. Surprise and disillusionment came over the officer's face. Turning, to my father, he said, "Peter Yakovlevich, I expected to see the luxurious flat of an American missionary, but here"—the inspector's hand described a semicircle in the air, and the surprise on his face changed to a sneer—"is poverty!"

The search was carried out. They took a Bible, a Gospel, personal letters, and photographs. Father had a bag of dried crusts ready and waiting. He put on warm clothing, said our last prayer together in the presence of the inspector, and Father was taken away . . .

We could hear the car, which had stood slightly to one side of the house, hooting as it moved off. I ran out into the yard behind the shed and wept. Terrible grief pierced my heart. I heard my mother calling me loudly, searching. "Mother, I don't want to live any longer!" My mother, weeping, led me away and soothed me.

After Father's arrest, the owner of the house refused to let us stay in the room. We faced the problem of lodging—long searches. Many believers refused us living quarters—they were afraid. At last, a believer, Alexandra Semirech, took us in. She was a simple, sincere sister. She had two teenage sons and a husband who was an unbeliever, an inveterate drunkard, and a terrible brawler. They lived not far from the Cossack bazaar along Pushkin Street. They owned one third of the house. Of their two rooms, Alexandra Ivanovna and her family took the larger, and the smaller they gave up to us. The owner of the house was almost always drunk. Sometimes during the night, a brawl would start up. Then mother and I would get out through the window and flee to neighbors.

Several more brothers were arrested together with my father. Among them was Father's friend Anton Pavlovich Martynenko, Butevich, the pastor of an Evangelical Christian community, and others. V.P., the former executive of the Far East Union of Christians-Baptists, was also arrested.

On Sundays, we took a parcel to prison for Father. In those days, Omsk prison was a long way out of town. However, in the '30s, the town grew considerably and surrounded the great four-storied bulk of the prison on all sides.

There was a long queue to the window where parcels were handed in. Everyone was bringing something to a loved one. Anxiously, they asked if he was alive, when he would be released, when the trial would be, and many other things. The answers were general and formal. But if they took the parcel, it meant he was alive and still there.

Not many people cried. Their tears had already been wept out and grief had hidden itself in the depths of sunken eyes. Some did cry—the "novices."

The parcels we brought were large, at Father's request, so he could share them with others. He was held in a cell with Siberian Tatars or Cossacks, I don't remember exactly, but with Muslims, not Russians. We sent him many rusks, boiled potatoes, onions, and sugar. It was almost a commune—they had all things in common. Father was the "trustee" in his cell, and the only Russian there. The Muslims took to him at once and helped him with a will to form a bond.

Before me are a few yellowed pages from a notebook. They contain short penciled letters in my father's hand from Omsk prison. Every line and every word of my father's is dear to me. How grateful I am to the Lord for preserving them! How much spiritual strength I derive from my father's sacred biblical precepts!

April 11th, 1936
My dear ones,

There is still no change in my case. Klimenko has been on a week's hunger strike for the second time. He has already been interrogated once. The procurator has promised to conclude the investigation by September 15th. But I don't think I believe that.

Tell our dear ones to pray that the Lord will strengthen the brethren and myself to be His faithful witnesses. It is doubtful that we shall be released, although our only crime is faithfulness to the Lord. I believe that the Lord can do anything. It is better to be with Him in prison than at liberty without Him.

Yours until death,
Father

October 1936
Dear L. and beloved G.

From September 26th, I was summoned twice a day to interrogation, and the investigation was concluded on October 5th.

The Lord strengthened me and gave me the power and the courage to confess Him. They have promised to pass my case over to the special board of the regional court. There is some hope that the trial will take place in November. According to the interrogator, there are twelve of us: A.P., Klimenko, Peter Ignatievich, Butkevich, the pastor of a community of Evangelical Christians and six others—I don't know who they are: but V.P. has been released because he was not active in the work of the community. The Lord is our defense.

The medical commission came: I have dilation of the heart muscles and a condition of the appendix. I pray the Lord to strengthen you physically and spiritually. Don't worry about me.

May God keep you!
Peter

November 15th
Greetings my dear L. and G!

I hope there will not now be long for us to wait until the trial, and then we will be granted a meeting. The case has now been passed to the special board of the regional court. I hope the trial will be held at the end of November or the beginning of December. Come to the trial. We will be granted a meeting there. The regional procurator and the special board can permit a meeting before the trial. I miss you very much, my darlings. I worry because I don't know how you are and what the state of your health is, Lydia. In my thoughts, I dwell with delight on happy moments spent with you. To my deep regret, there were not so very many of them . . .

The last seven months, which I have spent in this school of patience have taught me a great deal, I hope for my whole life. Don't worry about me; I am in good spiritual health and relatively so in body too. You can write to me here by post at the prison address: Investigation Block 3, cell No. 12.

Greetings to mother and all our dear ones. I kiss you affectionately,

Father
Vins P. Ya.

December 15th, 1936
My beloved darlings:

Today I have just (at four o'clock in the afternoon) received your precious letter of November 29th—this is the first letter. As I was reading it, the tears kept welling up in my eyes, and it cost an enormous effort of will to hide them from my comrades in the cell. But it was not because I was downhearted, but on account of your love for me, which shines through your letter. Your wish that I should not be downhearted entirely coincides with mine, and so far I have not been. The prison authorities treat me well. The comrades in the cell treat me very well. As in the interests of hygiene, we have marked off a corner for smoking, which all the smokers conscientiously observe. In a word, I live tolerably well, for no thefts or excesses are committed in our cell, and if you were with me, and moreover if we were free, then it would be quite all right. However, it is as it is, only don't worry about me. I would like just one thing, to be sentenced soon, for I don't expect to be released. The time of the trial is not yet known, but all the same, I hope it will take place soon.

I am very satisfied with Gosha's (Georgi's) behavior. I rejoice that I have such a fine obedient son growing up. I would like him to remain like that. I am sure the time will come when we shall be together once more.

I kiss you affectionately,

Your father
Cell No. 12

During his investigation, Father was summoned to a confrontation with V.P., who in the presence of the interrogator asked Father to confirm that he had carried out no spiritual work in Omsk and had generally stayed at home. Father confirmed this. V.P. was released, although his passivity did not save him later on: he was arrested again in 1937 and died in imprisonment.

The investigation lasted nine months. The accusation was constructed on the false evidence of two spiritually weakened believers. One of them worked as a caretaker, and the other was a housewife. Both were terribly intimidated and confused by the interrogator and signed any fabrications, even the most improbable. The main drift of these fabrications was that Father and others had allegedly engaged in anti-Soviet agitation in their sermons. Even at a confrontation with Father these cowed believers confirmed the lie thought up by the interrogator. It is true that they did not look him in the eye, as Father subsequently recounted.

On arriving home one day after taking Father a parcel, Mother undid a white sugar bag which Father had passed to her, and on the reverse side were described in indelible pencil in Father's hand both the confrontations and all that the above-mentioned witnesses had said. She told Alexandra Ivanovna Semirech about this.

This energetic sister, faithful to the Lord, visited both the false witnesses, who thought that no one would ever find out about their evidence. They were amazed their secret had been found out, although they did not know how.

This is what happened. Alexandra Ivanovna took another sister with her. They found the said brother, the caretaker, and told him that they wanted to talk to him about a very important matter. He led them into the garret of a large house. There they said to him, "At the confrontation with Peter Yakovlevich, you said this . . . !" They recounted all that he had said and that my father had replied. This brother had never expected such an exposure. He fell to his knees and repented loudly before God. Then he told them how he had been intimidated during the interrogation, threatened with arrest, and so on. He said, "I was very unhappy about my false evidence. I lost peace and rest in my heart. Now that I see the Lord has finally exposed me, I am ready even to go to prison, if only I can take back all I said."

They prayed and decided that at the trial he would tell only the truth. The other witness, the sister who was a housewife, came to a similar decision.

The trial took place at the end of 1936. It was held in the large hall of the regional court in Lenin Street. Relatives of the accused and some believers were present. In the hall stood solid church benches, taken at the time of the confiscation of a prayer house. The believers ran their hands lovingly over the backs of the benches, and said, "We can sit on our own benches one more time!"

The accused (eleven men) were cheerful and lively. They were accused under article 58.* Preaching about Christ was considered as anti-Soviet agitation. However, the witnesses, as one man, retracted their false evidence and openly recounted how they had been threatened and intimidated at the investigation.

Great discomfiture for the court! But it wanted to be objective: after all, the 1936 Constitution of the USSR had only just been published. The trial went on for a few days and ended with the release of all the accused on the signing of an undertaking not to leave the district. The case was passed to the NKVD for re-investigation.

At the end of the trial, the judge addressed my father, "You are a man with education, but you concern yourself with faith—dope!"

---

* Article 58 was included in the division of the Criminal Code dealing with "crimes against the State." Those charged under it were not recognized as political offenders, but treated as criminals. Its fourteen sections were widely applied in the 1930s to cover every aspect of life.

Interrupting the judge, Father replied, "I beg you not to insult our faith! Faith in God is the purpose of my life!"

Father was free!

Nine months had passed since the day of his arrest, but today there was joy, tears, and embraces. I was dragged into the hall too (I had not been admitted during the trial). Father had grown thin, his clothes smelt unpleasantly of prison, but what did I care about that, it was my daddy, my very own, my own! He lifted me up in his arms and said, "How big you are! Your legs reach right down to the ground!" Carefully, he set me down.

We all went home. Toward evening, a small group of believers gathered. Fervent prayers were addressed to our Heavenly Father. Then far into the night, Father told us about all he had been through.

LAST DAYS OF FREEDOM

After his release, Father began trying to find work. But everywhere he was turned down. Other brothers were in the same position. Then they formed a carpenters' team of fifteen men (all believers), and the whole team was contracted to a building office for work. Our family's material position improved slightly.

By that time, meetings in Omsk had been forbidden. The small prayer house behind the station was closed. But there were about a thousand believers in Omsk. Some of them began to leave. Some, frightened, stayed at home and grew spiritually cold.

Part of the brotherhood, my father among them, continued to visit believers and conducted small meetings. The doors of our house were scarcely ever closed. Every day believers kept coming for advice and for spiritual support. The owner of the house (an unbeliever) greatly respected Father and did not obstruct the visits.

Some people tried to frighten Father and his friend Anton Pavlovich with stories about the new wave of arrests of believers throughout the whole country—to this Anton Pavlovich replied with a smile, "Here we are guests! Soon we will go home again—to prison!" They used every day of freedom for preaching the Gospel and encouraging believers.

At this time, nearly all the churches and prayer houses throughout the country were closed. Thousands of Christians of different denominations were thrown into prisons and labor camps for their faith. I was constantly hearing that this brother had been arrested and that those had been searched. Husbands and sons, fathers and mothers, Bibles and Gospels were taken away.

And so I came into communion with the persecuted church of Christ in Russia!

I was full of joy to see Father at home, but I sensed it was only for a short while. Soon a new parting was in view. Once again, warm clothing was prepared, again rusks were dried.

One evening, I observed my parents cutting up a small Gospel into several parts and sewing it in sections into a coat collar, into the lining and into warm quilted trousers. Now eight years old, I understood it all: the parting was near.

Often Father would take me on his knees and the three of us would sing his favorite hymn, "I love Thy house, O Lord!" A Siberian snowstorm raged outside the windows, the wind howled drearily, but in our little room, it was warm and cozy. We were happy: Father was with us. I sang together with my father:

I love Thy house, O Lord,
The palace of Thy love.
I love the Church of people
Redeemed by Christ!

THIRD ARREST

One evening, after coming home from work, Father had his supper and went out visiting. Immediately after he had left, a car with NKVD agents drew up outside the house. They came inside and showed my mother a warrant for Father's arrest and for a search. Once more our last spiritual literature and letters were confiscated. The search was short. Meanwhile mother was preparing food for Father's journey.

Father came home late in the evening. He was very calm. We too were calm. We prayed, Father embraced me and mother for the last time, and we parted forever, or rather until our meeting in eternity before the Lord!

That same evening Martynenko and other believers were arrested. It was 1937 . . .

For a while, they accepted parcels from us, and we even saw Father. But how did we see him? Every free day Mother and I went to the prison building. (They had agreed on this earlier before the arrest.) On three sides, the prison was adjoined by quiet streets with little one-story wooden houses which had the traditional Russian benches at their gates. The first time we walked slowly along the streets around the prison. In one of the prison windows on the fourth floor, someone waved his arms. We could not see his face. But it was worth our appearing again opposite that window with the grille, so urgently did he wave. It was Father. From other cells, peoples' faces looked at us indifferently.

We sat down on a bench at the gates of one of the houses and looked at the window. As we approached, Father hailed us, vigorously gesticulating at the window. We sat for several hours and were happy that he could see us . . . But then they began to fix special boxes over the prison windows, which were open only on the upper side. They began fixing them on the lower stories. The window of Father's cell was not open for much longer.

One day, we came and saw there remained only a few windows without boxes, among them Father's window. He also knew that this was our last meeting. We looked at him for an especially long time. Periodically, he waved his hand. We want to preserve in our memories for our whole lives just the wave of his hand and the dim silhouette of his face. Father did not go away from the window for a long time. He kept looking and looking at us. This was our last meeting.

By the next day, boxes were hanging on all the windows of the prison. We stood in silence opposite Father's cell, mentally appealing to God, and went sadly home . . .

Farewell, Father, until our meeting before the Lord!

In the winter of 1937, large parties of prisoners were often driven in convoy past our house. Unshaven, lean faces. In dark clothes and with knapsacks on their backs, they walked along the roadway toward the station and looked avidly to either side, seeking their relatives and friends. I went out into the street and searchingly scrutinized the prisoners' faces; it seemed to me I was just on the point of seeing my father's face among them. But he was not among the convoy passing by. With a heavy heart, I went home.

Mother repeatedly made inquiries about Father's fate to different bodies. For a long time, there was no answer at all. Then, she was told that Father had been convicted by a closed court (the famous "*troika*"*) to ten years in labor camp without right of correspondence.

---

* *Troika* was the colloquial term for the Special Board, three-man boards of the People's Commissariat of Internal Affairs (NKVD) which had the power to sentence "socially dangerous" people without trial. They were abolished in 1953. "Troika" means "group of three."

Mother consoled me, saying, "When you grow up and you are eighteen years old, Father will come back!" But alas, more than one decade has passed now, and still he is not here.

He died on December 27th, 1943 at the age of forty-five in one of the Far East labor camps. Anton Pavlovich Martynenko and many others did not return either. God alone knows where their ashes lie.

Twenty years after father's death, on December 24th, 1963, by my mother's petition, father's case was reconsidered by the Omsk regional court. In view of the absence of *corpus delicti*, my father was posthumously rehabilitated!

Again and again, I re-read Father's short letters:

> Tell our dear ones to pray that the Lord will strengthen the brethren and myself to be His faithful witnesses.
>
> It is doubtful that we shall be released, although our only crime is faithfulness to the Lord.
>
> It is better to be with Him in prison than at liberty without Him!

In the short days of freedom, he loved to sing a hymn of the suffering brotherhood which was very widespread in the years before the war:

> For my suffering brothers—for mankind,
> Help me, God, to yield up everything,
> And from the abyss of sinful passions
> Raise me up to the eternal truth of heaven.
>
> For mankind, for mankind,
> Help me, God to yield up everything,

So that more swiftly and more bravely
I may save brothers who perish!

Over the last forty years, many thousands of believers have passed through the prisons and camps of our country. Their only "crime" is faithfulness to the Lord!*

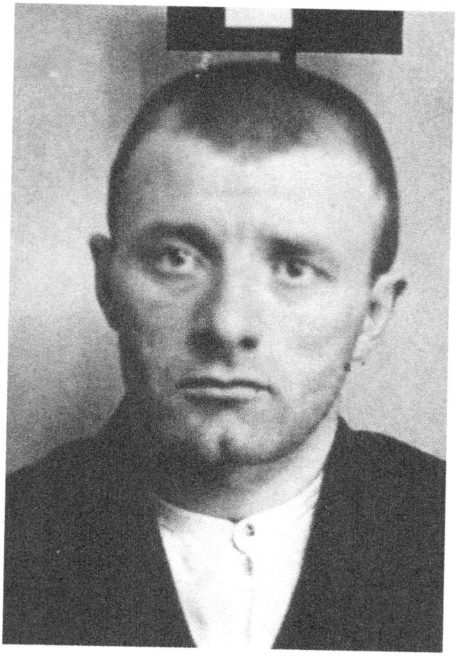

Photo of Peter Vins taken in 1937 in Siberia, the year he was executed.

*For several decades, Lydia and her son Georgi believed that Peter had died in 1943, as they had been told. In 1995, Georgi Vins was permitted to go to the KGB archives in Moscow and read the file the NKVD had kept on his father. Labeled "Top Secret," its pages revealed that the authorities executed his father with a bullet in August 1937 at the age of 39.

Nadia, Georgi, Natasha, Lydia (1955)

MY LABOR CAMP DIARY

POEMS AND REFLECTIONS WRITTEN IN PRISON 1966-1969*

Sometimes the reader
Observes it in poetry:
In truth it is the path of thorns
Of Russian Christians!
(From a poem by the Christian poet V.B.)

May 19th, 1966

Moscow. Lefortovo Prison—a KGB investigation cell in solitary confinement. Freedom, family, friends have remained far away. A month ago, my younger daughter took her first step . . .

I have also taken my first step—but into prison.

The cell door slammed . . .

When shall I see my dear children, my darling wife, and my aging mother again? The world has narrowed to four stone walls and

*Much of this section, "My Labor Camp Diary," is also in the Lighthouse Trails editon of Georgi's book, *Moscow Express.* Also, there is some slight variation in some of the wording due to the adjusted translating edits by Keston College in the 1970s.

a massive metal door. The prison window is painted white and guarded by a simple grille. At home in the Ukraine, it is spring, with an expanse of sky, an expanse of fields, forests, and rivers.

But here is a mute stone grave. My body is in captivity, and there are constant attempts from outside to work on my spirit, to humiliate and break it, and, if it were possible, to buy it.

Through the half-open ventilation window, crisscrossed by the grille, a small piece of rain-swept sky can be seen.

The sky is weeping. Is it not weeping for us, Christian prisoners, shut up within the gloomy walls of an ancient Russian prison?

Somewhere not far away is an open Orthodox church. In our exercise period on Sunday mornings, the muffled sound of the bell can be heard. The faith is still alive in Russia!

I walk up and down the cell. Six paces forward, six paces back. The cell is small for its quota of one or two prisoners.

Thoughts about my dear ones and thoughts about Christ—the Savior of the world. Only *He* gives freedom of spirit and real happiness. Christ gives the strength to withstand atheism!

I am not alone here. My brothers in the faith are in many neighboring cells. Even within these walls, almighty God is strengthening our faith and inspiring radiant hope in our hearts.

Christ is unconquerable!
The faith lives and grows stronger!
The Messiah is with us!
Our native Russia needs him!

On the tablets of my heart, I record the first lines of a poem. There is no pen or pencil or paper. Only the heart's remembrance.

The Messiah

Far away from the forests of Russia,
From her plains and rivers,
In Judea was born the Messiah,
The true holy man.

He was simple and accessible to the people,
His gaze breathed sympathy to men,
But in His speeches, He mercilessly exposed
Liars and tyrants of freedom.

He experienced suffering and tears,
And was crucified by a wicked mob.
Is it not for this that the birches weep
With their bright sap of early spring?

Is it not for these, as sacred tears,
That the heavens often pour down rain,
Is it not for this that in the songs of Russia
A smoldering melancholy lives?

Do not be sad, dear Nature,
Man, do not be cast down in soul!
On Golgotha is the beginning of the sunrise
Of a new life and happiness forever.

This life was crucified on crosses,
This happiness was burnt at the stake,
But O miracle!—Others arose
And bore it with faith in their hearts!

There is a land on earth—Russia,
There are true sons of God there,
Inconspicuous people, and homely,
But full of Christ's strength!

Faith in God like a mighty river
Flows through the broad plains of Russia.
Man's very best friend, Jesus
Summons the people to salvation!

May-June 1966
Moscow, Lefortovo prison

August 1966

The first weeks and months of imprisonment pass slowly by. Despite the very strict isolation of Lefortovo Prison, a link between the Christian prisoners is gradually established and functions successfully. I know about almost all the believers who are held here. All are cheerful and steadfast in their trials for the faith. There are now about thirty of us in the prison. Some have already been sentenced. Some have now had meetings with their relatives. My relatives are alive and well: my mother was present at one of the trials. I am told she was very sad. My darling mother!

Once again prison has visited you and me. Since you were twenty-three years old your life has been passed in the shadow of prisons and camps: first those of your husband, now those of your son. You have borne many griefs and partings on the thorny path of Russian Christians.

Do not be sad, my darling. Christ's victory is eternal! Christ is the Victor of death and hell, and even more of modern unbelief.

The investigation draws to its end. The trial will take place soon. There are two of us in this case: myself and Gennadi Konstantinovich Kryuchkov, a faithful servant of the Lord. He is unusually short, a modest and sincere brother with a great, unshakable faith in God's strength and might.

For what are we being tried? For free faith in Christ! In fact, it is not we who are on trial, but Christ! We are merely His twentieth-century disciples, and we are saying and doing nothing new. We continue to witness to the Gospel about the salvation of man and about eternal life in Christ.

Our interrogators, procurators, and judges have not come very far from those who participated in Christ's trial in the first century—they use the same methods: slander, falsehood, and hatred for God's truth.

There is no question of justice. Atheism, invested with power, creates tyranny.

I prepare for the trial . . . By now I have pencil and paper. My first thought: we are appearing here (before the court), not for robbery, not for rioting, not for gold, not for hooliganism.

The trial of Jesus Christ is continuing here today, the trial which was begun in the time of the Roman procurator in Judea—Pontius Pilate.

It is faith in the bright future of humanity that is on trial. Christ was calm, full of spiritual strength, and confident of the victory of the cause of the Gospel. His confidence is transmitted even to us.

These first thoughts are lying on the paper in verse. I alter and rewrite it many times, until I arrive at the definitive version.

The hall of the Moscow regional court. On November 30th, 1966 in my final address, I recite my poem.

They interrupt me several times. I omit the last couplet.

Not for Robbery

Not for robbery, nor for gold,
Do we stand before you.
Today here, as in Pilate's day,
Christ our Savior is being judged . . .

Holy Prophet from Nazareth,
Why are you being judged today?
Is it because you are the source of light,
Of love, of good, and of purity?

Is it because you made a gift of freedom
To sons of sin, to slaves of passions,
And revealed salvation to the peoples.
Through the love within yourself?

Once again abuse resounds,
Again slander and falsehood prevail;
Yet He stands silent, sorrowfully
Looking down on us poor sinners.

He hears the sorry threats,
He sees the trepidation of those people
Whose hands have gathered tears
Of children, wives, and mothers.

Forgetful of history's lessons,
They burn with desire to punish
Freedom of conscience and of faith
And the right to serve the Lord.

No! You cannot kill the freedom of belief;
Or shut up Christ in jail!

The examples of His triumphs
Will live in hearts He's saved.

A silent guard binds round
The friends of Christ with steel ring,
But Christ Himself inspires us
To stand serene before this court.

No rebel call has passed our lips,
No children offered as a sacrifice,
We preached salvation constantly,
Our message one of holy thoughts.

We call upon the church of Christ
To tread the path of thorns,
We summon to a heavenly goal,
We challenge perfidy and lies.

And so we stand before you,
Or rather, have been forced to come,
So you can learn the ways of God,
That sons of His stay true to Him.

That our faith is not legend,
Not a vestige of years gone by;
It is the radiance of immortality,
For us it is both life and light!

Fresh trials now and persecution
Will serve alone to strengthen faith
And witness God's eternal truth
Before the generations still to come.

Arise, new champions,
For the cause of Christ's truth!
Bear the Word of God boldly
To every corner of the land!

November 1966
Moscow, Lefortovo Prison

Early in the morning of the second day of the trial, I sketch out a few lines of verse in my cell. On the first day of the trial, one of the witnesses, a believer from the town of Prokopievsk, answered very well.

The judge asks, "Do you know the accused?"

The witness answers, "Yes, they are my brothers in the faith."

Judge: "Where did you meet them?"

Witness: "I have never met them before."

Judge: "Then why do you say that you know them?"

Witness: "I know them through the blood of Christ! They are Christians, and that is why they are under arrest."

This testimony deeply moved both myself and my friend.

Don't be alarmed! Anxiety begone!
Today I must face
A court of ungodly men
To defend the truth.

To defend those persecuted for the truth,
Those who have found life's meaning in Christ,
My own brothers and sisters
Through the blood poured out on the Cross!

November 30th, 1966
Moscow, Lefortovo Prison

February 16th, 1967. Moscow transit prison.

My last meeting with my wife.

Where will they send me?

February 19th, 1967. Evening.

I am referred to a transit cell. It is full of men, mostly Muscovites sentenced for hooliganism under the 1966 Decree.

Conversation is noisy. Everyone feels ready for the road. We are all preoccupied by one thing: where will we be taken, and will there be an amnesty? The convoy is supposed to be going to the east.

The guard shouts out the names of the prisoners (*zeks*) through a window in the door and issues each man with rations for the journey: bread, sugar, herring. But he does not give everyone the same.

According to the amount of bread they receive, the *zeks* can estimate approximately the duration of their convoy and the district: one loaf of bread lasts two days, which means the convoy is to the Urals; two loaves mean Siberia, Tyumen and beyond. I receive one loaf of bread, thirty grams of sugar, and two herrings.

February 20th

We are sent off on the convoy. It is early morning, and cold. A covered lorry—a "black raven"—is waiting for us in the prison yard.

We are driven to the sidings of Kursk station and quickly get out of the "raven." Around us are the guards: soldiers with machine guns and convoy dogs. It is the first time I have seen them so close. The dogs become nervous at the sight of us and strain their leashes in our direction.

We are taken to an ordinary luggage van—but inside are sleepers made into cells. On the corridor side is a metal grid of thick wire and a latticed door. This is a *zek* carriage. We are led into it and assigned to cells. Our carriage is shunted around the sidings for a long time and is finally coupled to one of the passenger trains.

We are setting out from Moscow. Farewell to the capital.

There are fifteen or sixteen men in the sleeper cell. I sleep sitting up, leaning against the wall.

February 22nd

We spend the night in Perm. We get out of the train. Once more, we are met by dogs, guards, and a "black raven." Toward morning, we are brought into Perm Prison. There is the usual search, and then at five o'clock in the morning we find ourselves in an overcrowded cell, crammed full of men. They are sleeping everywhere: both on the plank beds and underneath them, and simply in the passageway on the cement floor. We have difficulty in finding a place on the floor.

Reveille is at six o'clock in the morning.

The air is terribly stuffy. Tobacco smoke chokes our lungs.

In the cell is an elderly man who will be released in ten days' time. I ask him to forward a letter to my family at one of a number of addresses once he is free. I put into an envelope several poems I have written in Lefortovo. Subsequently, I will learn that the letter reached my family safely.

The Tiaga forests in the desolate Ural mountains

February 27th

We rejoin the convoy. We are being taken to Solikamsk in the northern Urals.

February 28th, Solikamsk.

From the station, we are taken by lorry to the transit prison. There is no railway beyond here. But our way lies farther—to the north. We wait for the convoy for a long time. We are held in a small cell, very cramped and stuffy.

March 14th

The convoy, at last, on three lorries.

There are three open lorries with an escort and dogs. Before us are 200-250 kilometers of taiga roads.

Somewhere here in 1930, my father was driven on foot in a convoy along the roads of the taiga. Perhaps along these very same roads?

We pass through several ancient Russian towns. The last of them is Cherdyn.

Toward evening we are brought into one of the taiga labor camps on the bank of the River Kama. But for us this camp is only a transit point. Our way lies still further.

March 21st

The convoy has lasted a week. We set off early in the morning. In the evening, we arrive at a timber-felling camp named "Chapechanka."

Here winter is still in full spate. There is snow in abundance. All around are the backwoods and the taiga. For tens of kilometers, there is not even one village . . . This is the North.

Although it is rather late, I write my son a New Year poem which I composed during the journey. I also finish a poem for my daughter.

Speed forth, reindeer,
From distant villages,
Bear greetings to my dear ones!
A New Year greeting
With the love of the Lord,
And the light of future happiness.

From distant villages
Reindeer, fly forth,
Bear a greeting to my loved ones!
Tell them: In the rigors
Of his wanderings for the Word,
This prisoner is warmed by love.

Through the storms of the North
To the blue sky of heaven
The way is paved with suffering.
My son, never forget
Men who are living examples
Of faith in action!

March1967
Perm region "Chapechanka"

A Letter From My Mother
May 17th, 1967

My warmest kisses, my son. How is your health? I talk to you constantly and am full of anxieties and worries, but I have not been able to write. I had already received your precious letter before our meeting. It was a consolation for me in my old age. How often we fail to understand old people—their weaknesses and loves. In old age, everything returns to your memory and gives you pain. However, man comes to Earth to pass through and leave.

The whole trouble lies in the passing through. The honest road is a hard one. I am not talking about financial honesty, but spiritual honesty, the ability to look directly, to keep the soul from becoming distorted, to act at no time for personal gain. Many have traveled this road, but compared to the general mass, they are a handful. They are admired more after they have died, but whilst alive, they are thought eccentric, to say the least. The spirit and motto of recent times is this: take all you can from life. Very quickly such souls, like butterflies, scorch their wings in the fire, and for the remaining years of their lives, they grovel in futility and deformity.

Your road is hard. I know, bitter moments of loneliness come, when it seems you are on the point of falling beneath the weight of the cross. Do not despair, but rather be assured at such times that the sun is shining behind the storm clouds. You are still young, and you will survive and even forget this suffering.

But do carry away with you these lessons for life. It is good to cultivate self-control, to acquire the fine quality of self-restraint, even when they undeservedly touch the holiest and noblest parts of your soul. This is the most vital thing in life. I am not talking about slave-like submissiveness. This robs a man of his dignity as a person and as an heir to eternal life.

I would like to tell you much about my pains and joys, but I do not have the opportunity. Meanwhile, all is well. The gardens are past full blossom. The days fly headlong toward the future, and we fly along with them. What will your yield be? As it is written, "their works do follow them!" (Revelation 14:13)

The anniversary of your imprisonment is in a day's time. It is a sad and bitter day. Be strong, my child; you acted nobly that day, like your father's son. The Lord will surround you with His light and take away all heaviness from your heart. "Thou, which hast shewed me great and sore troubles, shalt quicken me again, and shalt bring me up again from the depths of the earth. Thou shalt increase my greatness, and comfort me on every side" (Psalm 71:20-21).

May God preserve you! Amid all adversities may He protect your soul from evil and guard your life in complete wellbeing. I pray for this constantly, with tears in my eyes. Let us entrust ourselves to Him, the Guardian of our souls. Let us set our hope on Him. Our breath and our life are in His hands.

> He knows how the journey wearied us,
> How little we have rested, how we have carried our cross.
> He will take away our burden when he comes,
> The time of bliss approaches—the Lord draws near.

Your father and I once sang this song, but now I sing it with you, and there in eternity, we shall sing it together, all three. I kiss you and greet all the father's children. "Yea, I have loved thee with an everlasting love: therefore with lovingkindness have I drawn thee" (Jeremiah 31:3).

Your mother.

I noticed in the camp how the families of many of those who found themselves in prison would break up. You would see how first one man would receive an official divorce from his wife, and then another's wife would write that she was no longer waiting for him and had a new family. It was hard to watch the increasing spiritual suffering of these men.

Yes, it is certainly hard to live without the Lord! However, the example of faith and steadfastness of the wives of the Christian prisoners called forth the wonder and admiration of many other prisoners. Even in their letters, the believers' lives not only did not reproach their husbands with the increase of their family troubles in connection with their arrest, but, on the contrary, they encouraged them, and urged them to be faithful to the Lord until death!

And when the wives of our prisoner brothers came to visit them in the distant northern camps, the whole camp and the entire guard used to talk about it, often with admiration.

In the "Chapechanka" camp in the northern Urals, I spent three months together with two brothers in the faith, both sentenced for confessing their belief in Christ.

One of these brothers, Fyodor Vladimirovich Makhovitsky, a pastor of the Leningrad Evangelical Christian-Baptist Church, worked until his arrest as a metal worker in the Kirov factory. The father of seven children, he was sentenced at the end of 1966 to two years in labor camp and was sent off to the northern Urals.

Fyodor Makhovitsky

Immediately, within two weeks of brother Makhovitsky's arrival in the camp, his wife, Klavdia Alexandrovna, arrived from Leningrad for a meeting with him and brought him a parcel. This was an unusual sight in the history of this northern camp lost in the midst of the Ural forests. On the whole, it was relatives living near the Urals who came to visit the prisoners.

The other brother, a Circassian by nationality, was Konshaubi Bekirovich Dzhangetov, the father of six children. He was sentenced in the autumn of 1966 in the town of Cherkassk in the northern Caucasus to three years in labor camps.

A former Muslim, Konshaubi* had come to faith in Christ at the age of nineteen. He had to endure much and to bear the persecution of his unbelieving relatives. However, his faith in Christ did not weaken but became even stronger and firmer. Now he was enduring new persecution, but this time from atheists. I will not forget his joy and his fervent prayer of thanks to the Lord when his wife Tonya came to visit him in the North, undeterred by a distance of several thousand kilometers. His happiness knew no bounds. During brother Konshaubi's meeting with his wife, brother Fyodor Vladimirovich and I remained not far from the meeting barracks, and our dear sister in the Lord, Tonya, waved her hand to us through the window and gave us a friendly smile. She was a true help-meet to her prisoner husband.

Within three months, we were once more on the prisoners' trail. The reason for this was our Christian life in the camp. In the barracks where we lived, we three prayed openly by our plank beds. We talked just as openly about God with the people around us. The prisoners, and also the soldiers and officers of the guard, showed great interest and asked us numerous questions: about the reason for our arrest, about our faith, about the Bible, about God. We tried to give thorough Christian answers to all these

Konshaubi Dzhangetov

* Georgi Vins writes about Konshaubi in the book *Konshaubi: Free on the Inside*. Used copies can be found online. Konshaubi's story is also featured in the DVD film, *Captive Faith* (carried by Lighthouse Trails).

questions. Some of the prisoners stopped smoking and swearing, and even began to pray. All this greatly troubled not only the local camp authorities, but also Moscow.

The camp commandant once said among a group of officers, and it was reported to us, "Another six months and half the camp will become Baptists!" Of course, he was greatly exaggerating, but the atheists' degree of alarm was very high.

At the end of June 1967, a special commission from Moscow arrived in our distant taiga camp. In the most categorical way, they forbade us to pray and to talk about God. But we could not submit to these demands.

One of the brothers told the colonel who headed the commission: "We cannot cease to pray and to talk about God. This is our life. And if you have torn us away from our families and from our own homes and brought us to the North so that we should stop praying and believing—it won't happen. Even here we shall pray by our bunks and serve our God!"

A few days later, on July 6th, brother Makhovitsky and I were sent off on a convoy. Brother Dzhangetov was left behind.

We said farewell to our dear Konshaubi, and it was hard to part.

Indeed, "Behold, how good and how pleasant it is for brethren to dwell together in unity," especially in chains! (Psalm 133: 1)

On the day of our departure, Fyodor Makhovitsky's wife paid him a second visit, together with their seven-year-old son. They were allowed a short, two-hour meeting, and then the convoy.

Fifty kilometers along a narrow gage railway. We were transported in a *zek* carriage; and in the neighboring carriage, as a passenger, was sister Klavdia with her son Misha.

The locomotive with its two carriages moved slowly: there were trains carrying timber in front. There were frequent stops. Then sister Klavdia and Misha would come to the window of our carriage, and we would talk for a long time, thanks to our kind escort.

This fifty-kilometer journey took a whole day. With the permission of the escort, seven-year-old Misha several times supplied us with tomatoes or white bread.

After this, our way lay along the Kama, the great northern river. We were put into the hold of a motorized barge intended for transporting prisoners; and, accompanied by an escort and guard dogs, we set sail. The northern river was beautiful in summer, broad and full. The taiga came right up to the water's edge and was reflected in it. It was a quiet, warm, sunny day. From the open hold of the barge, I breathed in the fragrance of the taiga forest with delight and gazed with stirring emotion at the expanse of river that had opened up and at the freedom that was so near, and at the same time so far away. We sailed down the river as far as the small northern town of Bondyug, and then we were transferred to an open lorry and taken to Solikamsk where the transit prison was situated.

In the prison, we were put in a cell which had just been treated with insect powder. After the pure air of the river, infused with the resinous aroma of conifers, here there was a terrible stench of DDT powder hanging in the air. One could not breathe. It was like that until evening.

And then, suddenly, I was summoned to a meeting with my wife.

I don't understand! How did she get here! Perhaps there has been a mistake?

It turned out that my wife had gone to meet me in the camp, but while changing trains not far from there she met sister Klavdia, who told her that we were being taken by convoy to Solikamsk. My wife immediately changed direction and arrived in the town even earlier than I, together with sister Klavdia. They set about searching for us.

So now we had a two-hour meeting. How joyful I felt at seeing the dear, beloved face of my faithful wife. We prayed in the presence of the guard. And we talked a great, great deal.

The guard turned out to be a good man. He was an Uzbek. After the meeting, when he was conducting me across the prison yard, he asked, "Why did you take so few parcels?" he asked. "You should have taken all that your wife brought!"

I thanked him for his kind attitude and his sympathy.

The next day we were once more on the convoy. The prisoners were led out of the gates of the transit prison. A lorry with guards was waiting for us.

Our wives and Misha were standing not far off. They waved their hands when they saw us and blessed us for our new and unknown journey.

Dear help-meets of Christian prisoners! You are always with us: our prisons, convoys, and camps have passed through your hearts as well! You have mourned over them many times. Every step of our convicts' journey was accompanied by your prayers. You did everything in your power to lighten our lot.

Esfir Yakovlevna Zakharova, with a baby in arms and carrying a parcel, traveled from the distant Siberian village of Prokopievsk across the whole country to a camp in the northern Caucasus for a meeting with her husband. Her husband, P. F. Zakharov, was from 1966 to 1969 serving his third prison sentence for confessing his faith in Christ.

One day, having come all this distance, Esfir Yakovlevna spent several hours in tears begging the camp governors to permit a meeting, which they refused her. But the Lord heard her entreaties . . . and she saw her husband. This faithful wife of a Christian prisoner died not long ago.

Lydia Vasilevna, the wife of brother Kryuchkov, regularly traveled from Moscow to see her husband in a distant Siberian camp in Chitinskaya region. At that time, she had eight children! I do not have the means to describe everything and to list all the wives of our prisoner brothers who supported and strengthened their husbands' spirits.

A hundred years ago the Russian poet Nekrasov described the heroic deeds of the wives of the Decembrists,[3] who left their dear ones, their fathers and mothers, and paying no attention to deprivations and difficulties, traveled to their suffering husbands in cold, grim Siberia.

Who will describe the heroism of the wives of Christian prisoners of our brotherhood, who from the time of Voronin and Pavlov (in the '70s of the last century) right up to our times share partings, sorrows, and wanderings with their husbands for the name of Christ, and comfort and encourage the heralds of the Gospel?

Who will describe how the wife of Odintsov, Alexandra Stepanovna, made her way in 1938 to her husband in exile in the distant taiga village of Makovskoye in Krasnoyarsk territory? Later, after his martyrdom in prison, she waited for long years until the Lord should take her also to meet Nikolai Vasilievich who was so dear to her heart. What did she think over and experience in all those years? Only the Lord knows!

In 1933, Varvara Ivanovna Ananina, the wife of a well-known spiritual worker in Siberia, came from Siberia for a meeting with her husband in a camp in Medvezhegorsk in Karelia. Subsequently, she also, together with her husband, shared an obscure death in the camps.

Anna Petrovna, the wife of Ivanov-Klyshnikov, served eleven years in the camps, and so did many, many others.

Their heroism in the faith is written in the Book of Life before the throne of the Almighty! And in His own time, the Lord will bear witness about them before everyone! I have written a poem dedicated to the wives of Christian prisoners. It was thought out while I was still in Lefortovo.

To Prisoners' Wives

They that sow in tears shall reap in joy. (Psalm 126:5)

Prisoners' wives! To Christ be praise and honor
And worship world without end
For the radiant Gospel news
And for love and mercy to man!

In Christ's eyes is the light of good and truth,
In His words is consolation for the heart,
But His hands bear the trace of the torments and tortures
Which brought us eternal salvation.

Above Russia, from the Finnish shores
To the oceans of the Far East,
Resounds the summons of God's powerful words,
And the burning love of the great prophet.

He alone is capable of giving happiness,
Giving healing from the plague of sin.
He sent us to proclaim immortality,
Although prison and persecution were waiting for us.

Prisoners' wives! To Christ be praise and honor
For your courage in severe ordeals!
The Lord be your help in enduring separation
And in preserving the call of heaven.

The Lord be your help in bringing up your little ones
In the love of Christ, in humble forbearance;
In passing on all your strength of feelings and faith
And in teaching the treasured commandments.

In prison cells and distant camps
We pray for you and believe in the power of God,
That faith will not be slain, will not be imprisoned in
chains, Will not be suborned, will not be subverted by
falsehood.

Our persecutors, hearing about Christ,
Seeing our life and our faith,
Will thirst for spiritual beauty
And will follow our example.

Above Russia, from the northern seas
To the places warmed by the southern sun,
Is borne the song of the happiness of men
Who have found in Christ their Saviour and friend!

1966-1967

In Solikamsk, we were taken to the station in lorries and then once more into a zek carriage.

The journey was not far—to Kizel; and there I and brother Makhovitsky parted.

July 26th, 1967

I arrived in a timber-felling camp named "Anyusha," where I was held until the day of my release.

The first six months in the "Anyasha" camp were especially grim. During the lengthy daily marches from the camp to our place of work constructing the permanent way for a narrow-gage railway, I meditated a great deal on His Word and conversed in my thoughts with God. In the evenings, I transferred my thoughts to paper.

Meditations of a Prisoner

From your youth, you stood up for truth
Singer of good and eternal salvation . . .
Now here is the end of your labors—
The desolate taiga and the cordoned-off zone.

The crush of convoys and transfers . . .
A cement floor is now the poet's bed.
Instead of air—stench and stuffiness;
The world has shrunk to the walls of a cell.

You affirmed humanism and happiness
And summoned sons of unbelief to the light;
You preached the deathless ideal
And exposed vice and hypocrisy.

Well, how is it now? . . . Have dreams dispersed,
The hopes of youth, and rainbow day-dreams?
Convoy dogs, not flowers, surround you,
And biting frosts replace poetry!

But through the howling of the snowstorm,
The song of faith and love resounds in your breast as before,
And a voice says: "Go more boldly
Along the path of faithfulness to the great goal!"

Good and truth will conquer evil,
Darkness will disappear before the Son of the resurrection,
Dungeons will collapse, and their steel finery
Will be given to museums as exhibits!

October-November 1967
"Anyusha" Corrective Labor Camp

Two Letters From My Mother

October 4th, 1967

I send you my mother's blessing. May God give you wisdom to bear your cross in meekness and humility. May He give you strength to endure all things. May He also send you physical strength. My visit, together with the joy of actually seeing you, left a deep imprint on my aging heart. The shores of the other life which is not of this Earth are closer and closer. Much is being reappraised, much is drawing closer.

One thing does not pass, but ever and again powerfully floods the spirit: it is the same thing which from early youth compelled me to decline a brilliant personal career and now, at the time when old age and infirmity are overcoming me, is stirring and restoring me to life. This is the suffering of our multinational people—the sight of these young fallen sinners and criminals fills my soul with even more pity. It seems as though Christ's voice is heard in the distance as well as nearby, saying, "Give them something to eat."

I have seen faces twisted with evil become human on hearing a kind word. What a great task it is to rouse man from the animal state into which he has fallen. I know very well, my dear child, how difficult it is to do this now; this is why my heart is in deep sorrow. I think that He who created man in His own image and likeness suffers even more. And you are reckoned among the wicked. Who can fathom the depths of your mother's suffering? But He knows the way that I take. And your way also. He says, "My thoughts are not your thoughts." Trusting in these words calms one's soul.

Your grandmother Masha dreamt constantly of seeing you at home so you could bury her, but she did not wait long enough. I am awaiting your return home, I want to believe, as I have done all my life, in the triumph of good. I am waiting as ever for the awakening of human feeling and truth; I see humanity in everyone and do not want to let myself think that falsehood is victorious. May it be done to you according to your faith! Will my eyes see this? I do not know. It is a fine thing to remain unembittered by life's sufferings, to carry forth the brilliant ray of youth through life's storms. You are still young and have the whole of your life before you. How I would love to see your bright soul shining in your eyes with hope and faith! Oh my dear child! May God keep you in His powerful hand. I wish you peace in your soul.

Warm kisses.
Your mother.

October 25th, 1967

My dear child! I had a talk with Nadya after her meeting with you and am in anguish that you have grown so much weaker. Do not hide your state of health from me in the future. We shall go on believing that you will soon be home, but if not, we shall echo the words of the three young men, Shadrach, Meshach, and Abednego. As for my own health, do not take it to heart—the Lord will watch over me. For He leads us not by authority, but by faith.

> Friends! Where are you now? On what foreign shore
> Has an angry wave washed you up?
> With what audacity, what arrogance,
> Has it carried you above the fearful, seething chasm?

Your life is now clothed in a disgraceful shroud,
Your native shores are covered by a dark mist,
But your heart with its former avidity and fervor
Begs for endearments and welcome.

You must believe that these endearments
Fill the grieving hearts of your relatives and friends.
Although you are hidden away, numerous eyes
Watch over you and the bailing waves.

Not you alone, but your fathers and grandfathers
Endured and conquered the terrible tornado;
Once the confused Simon was drowning in it,
And his friends of little faith were suffering troubles.

Do not lose heart, brother, do not be terrified,
Let the terrible tornado exert all its ferocity,
The Savior Himself will rebuke it, as He did before,
For He is with us, my friend, so be strong and
do not be dismayed.

If you could become physically stronger, I would be greatly comforted. May the heavens preserve you from any harm whatsoever so that you can be at home among us again. A heavenly angel counts our tears and collects drop after drop in the cup of suffering. Look after yourself and may the Lord look after you. May He send you good sense. My warm kisses and blessing.

Your mother.

In January 1968, the state of my health worsened abruptly. Sometimes I thought that perhaps the end had already come.

But I wanted to be in the ranks of the warriors for the faith of Christ until my last breath. I begged the Lord to strengthen me.

How to die . . . one must also know this . . .
Not as a crushed, pitiful worm,
Not as a slave, not daring to dare—
But as a fighter against unbelief!
So that as I go along the narrow road
I will give myself to Christ with my whole soul
And never fraternize in the slightest
With injustice, perfidy and evil.

Hoisting the sail of radiant faith,
I shall race to my longed-for homeland,
And look into the eyes of Christ,
Who has stretched out His hand to life!
I shall say with a smile to my dear ones:
"My darlings . . . but tears . . . are not needed!
I shall wait in heaven for you,
The conquerors of death and hell!"

In the vivid light of eternal day
Jesus Himself will embrace me,
And no one, my friends, will ever
Take away from me eternal life!

January 1968
"Anyusha" Corrective Labor Camp

I have not seen my aging mother for a long time. How is she? I have heard that she is under threat of imminent arrest for petitioning for prisoners. If only I could manage to cheer her up. I pray for her . . .

February 1968

The last month of winter. But here it is still a long way to spring. The forest and the camp lie under huge snowdrifts. All the roads have been blocked by a snowstorm.

Soon it will be my mother's birthday—March 30th. I write her a poem. But how can 1 send it to her?

Recently, the link with the outside world has been somewhat hampered, and I cannot send it through the camp post. I wait for an opportunity.

Then on March 29th, I am told that my mother and my elder daughter have come on a visit to me. Is this not a miracle and God's answer to my prayers and apprehensions?

On March 30th, her birthday, we are granted a twenty-four-hour meeting. I read her the poem and how much to the point it is!

To My Mother

I would like to embrace you,
To look into your kind eyes,
To say a heart-to-heart word
To make the dusk of night disperse.

I would like to set your mother's heart
At rest by my return . . .
For the two of us to weep together over father,
Who bore torture for the faith.

Rest assured that your son has murdered no one,
Has not robbed them, nor brought them harm
He has loved Russia like a mother,
And wished her good and happiness.

Outside the window a blizzard has risen,
Snowing up the prison barracks;
Around there is only snow and more snow,
And the limitless expanse of taiga.

Winter has blocked all the roads . . .
Freedom appears only in dreams at night . . .
Only faith, as radiant as before,
Becomes stronger in God with the years!

February 1668
"Anyusha" Corrective Labor Camp

I love you, my earthly homeland, my Russia!

I love your austere natural beauty, the boundless expanse of your fields, the quiet of your forests, the calm majestic flow of deep rivers, the reverie of blue lakes But most of all, I love my people—the soul of Russia! Your grim history, so full of suffering, is close to my heart.

But I rejoice: Christ loves you!

He died for you also, for your people, my Russia! For the span of a thousand years, He has sent to your villages and towns His heralds of truth, of good, of salvation and eternal life!

Many have tried to hide from you the life-giving light of Christ's love, or to distort beyond recognition the truth of the Gospel. They are innumerable: princes and boyars,[4] Tsars and nobles, formalistic churchmen, and modern atheists.

But who can separate you, my own Russia, from the love of Christ? At all times you had sons who in the most improbable conditions witnessed to Christ! You need Christ, my homeland, and especially today . . .

The Lord will never leave you!

My Love and My Song is Russia

A bleak land of forests and snow . . .
Garlands of snow tenderly embrace the firs . . .
Between its snow-covered banks the taiga river
Dreams of spring and the April floods.

The white sails of the clouds across the sky
Bear a gift of great snows to the south.
On frosty days I whisper with tears in my eyes:
"My love and my song is Russia!"

The time will come: the rays of spring will melt the snow,
And the tree-tops in the forest will straighten;
The taiga streams will run
To bow in greeting to the great rivers.

The river banks will turn green
And the wind will play above the waves,
The meadowlands will be clothed with children,
Like lush, bright flowers.

A flock of cranes descending to a stream
Will cry out in greeting to its native haunts;
On a spring day, I whisper rapturously:
"My love and my song is Russia!"

Accustomed from childhood to bear misfortune,
I have endured partings, waited for meetings.
Protectively, I bore my dream
Of your happiness, my native land.

Believing in a supreme Love,
Which comes to us across the storm of ages,
Today I repeat again and again
That man's happiness is in Christ alone.

For your happiness I am ready to give up
My whole life and my young strength;
To say with joy as I die:
"My love and my song is Russia!"

The camp is situated among the majestic forests of the western Urals on the bank of the small taiga River Anyusha, which has given its name to the camp. It is a beautiful place in both winter and summer.

The beauty of nature is overshadowed by the melancholy sight of the camp, blighted by barbed wire, the barking of the convoy dogs, and the black reefers of the prisoners.

All this is so unnatural amid the enchanting natural beauty of the Urals.

The spring nights are poetic . . .

The spring forest murmurs even with light breaths of wind and is echoed by the deep spring river, born in the taiga. The camp zone is asleep, except for the guards. I go out of the barracks and listen to the voices of spring.

Somewhere far away is my home—the Ukraine, which is so dear to my heart. It is the homeland of my wife and our children, and now it is my homeland too. The last twenty years of my life are linked in the most intimate way with the Ukraine and with the dear Ukrainian Evangelical-Baptist brotherhood.

Good news from my friends in the Ukraine has arrived in the camp. They are praying and waiting for me.

In the summer and autumn of 1968, KGB officials were constant visitors to the camp. I was summoned to conversations lasting many hours. They suggested, cautiously at first, and then quite blatantly, that I should collaborate with them against the church. There were threats, and also offers of an early release. But at what a price! The fee for an early release was betrayal of God and His works. At the end of September, I took no food for ten days, demanding that the KGB should leave me in peace. After my hunger-strike, I wrote a poem addressed to my persecutors.

Letter From My Mother

December 8th, 1968

I send you best wishes for Christmas and for the coming New Year. The Lord be with you!

In these triumphant days, when the whole world rejoices, how good it is to feel that you are not alone! He who created worlds and the whole universe was incarnate in miniature as a child. How great is His love for us fallen sinners. Never and nowhere does He leave us alone. Invisible, He is with us, and with you also.

As the New Year approaches, I wish above all else that you may have inner strength so that you can overcome all difficulties and not be downhearted. "O thou afflicted, tossed with tempest, and not comforted, behold, I will lay thy stones with fair colors, and lay thy foundations with sapphires. And I will make thy windows of agates, and thy gates of carbuncles, and all thy borders of pleasant stones" (Isaiah 54:11-13). What tender consolation. Incline your head, as John once did, upon Jesus' breast, that He might be close to you. For with Him a weary spirit lacks nothing.

Some are already coming back home, having finished their sentences—rejoicing, spiritually grown up, courageous. Others are taking their places. Such is the path of Christianity. But yet a little while, a very little while, and He who approaches will come, He will not delay.

Your mother.

I often reflect on our Christian young people. Their spiritual birth is closely linked with the spiritual struggle of our brotherhood for the faith in Christ. Things are very difficult for Christian young people in our country. All the forces of atheism are directed against them. But I am glad for the young generation of Christians: they love Christ with their whole soul and follow Him selflessly.

To Young Captains of the Faith

For young captains of the faith,
Making their way to heaven,
I wish for faith without measure
And for courage to strengthen their hearts.

On the way will be winds of persecution,
A deceptive lull, like running underground,
Rocks of doubt underwater,
And the oppressive mist of unbelief.

But for those who are taught by Christ
To subdue the elements by strength of faith,
The sun of victory will shine
Through the gloomiest clouds.

At the sight of the wide sea
Of human tears and sorrows,
Do not desert people languishing in grief
Who have forgotten God!

Captains! Hold the banner higher!
The banner of God's radiant love!
Bring to life on the plains of humanity
The bright flame of the Good News.

For young captains of the faith,
Making their way to heaven,
I wish for faith without measure
And for courage to strengthen their hearts!

March 1969
"Anyusha" Corrective Labor Camp

Lukyanov prison in Kiev (photo taken in 1900)

FREEDOM IS NOT FOR IDLENESS

The end of my sentence is approaching. They try to frighten me with a new sentence. They say I will not reach my home: that they will arrest me again on the way there, and so on.

Many officials come for conversations.

Before me is freedom. But freedom for what? For inactivity? Or for new labor in the vast field of the Gospel?

I am not set free alone. My closest friends in the faith are also being released.

I write down: freedom is not for idleness.

Freedom Is Not for Idleness

Freedom is not for idleness,
The virgin soil of spiritual labors is waiting for us,
At the springtime thaw there is gaiety in the air,
And the cornfields are awaking from sleep.

The morning of Christ's Resurrection
Stirs the breast with a surplus of new strength,
And the message of the Gospel sounds afresh
Of Him who awoke souls to life.

In persecuted churches are triumphal meetings,
Many have tears of joy in their eyes,
And an everlasting confession of God
Burns with flaming love in their hearts.

My friends, I know: for Christ
You have passed in bonds along a grim path,
Even now you are ready dauntlessly
To go for the faith into distant places.

Freedom is not for idleness,
Service for men has become our aim,
We are called to bear good news.
Service for God—our happiness and honor!

April 1969
"Anyusha" Corrective Labor Camp

Return

I stand once more on the family threshold,
I breathe the flagrance of the fields of home.
The hard road is left far behind,
The road of convoys and taiga camps.

I embrace my children who have grown so much,
My darling wife and my dear old mother.
And in my hair, grown gray on convoys,
The snows of Russia gleam as a memory.

And He who is the nearest and dearest of all,
Who is the corner stone of our life,
Who increases our strength in the battles of the faith,
Watches over us from heaven with a gentle smile!

May 1969
Ukraine

MY MOTHER'S IMPRISONMENT

She hath done what she could. (Mark 14:8)

On December 1st, 1970, my mother was arrested in Kiev. It happened in the evening when she was in the house with my youngest children. After she had dressed and gotten ready to leave, my eldest daughter came home. The children's grandmother was very calm and cheerful. She prayed with her grandchildren and left the house accompanied by policemen.

The first snow had fallen, forming a soft carpet over the earth, earth so rich in tears and sorrow. The tall pine forest mother loved so much, which came right up to the town, looked down pensively upon the bustling people in military uniform, helping the old woman into the "black raven." Her beloved forest bade her farewell.

The children ran out into the streets without their coats and cried quietly. An ambulance stood next to the police car. It escorted the detainee to the prison.

My darling mother! Thirty-three years ago, you saw your husband—my father—off on his last prisoner's journey; and now my children have seen you off!

It is hard for me to realize that you are in prison! You are old and sick, living under such a burden of suffering.

My own dear! Oh, if only I were allowed to change places with you.

What crime have you ever committed?

In your old age, you stood up in defense of those persecuted for their faith.

"If thou forbear to deliver them that are drawn unto death, and those that are ready to be slain" (Proverbs 24:11). This is the call of God's Word.

Confronted by injustice and human suffering, every honest individual is obliged to speak out. This right belongs especially to the mother, the Christian mother. And you fulfilled your maternal Christian duties to the utmost of your strength.

Your persecutors could not forgive you for this! They made many different efforts to bring you to silence. They became convinced that your mother's heart was anxious not only for the fate of your son, who was victimized by atheism. Your heart was wider; for the grief of orphans and widowed Christians was your own grief, and the tears of those persecuted for the faith were your tears. It was then that the persecutors decided to throw you also into prison.

They naively assumed that by taking you and imprisoning you in darkness, every voice defending persecuted Christians would fall silent.

But the voice speaks on.

Through a thousand mouths . . .

It is heard at the child's cot where little children pray for their father, languishing behind bars for God's truth.

This voice is heard in the continual prayers of God's people. It is heard also in every signature written in defense of the persecuted and in each courageous testimony to God's truth before persecutors.

This voice will not be stifled.

It is hard for me, as a son, to realize you are in prison and to bear separation from you. I am even deprived of correspondence with you. I am deprived of the opportunity of cheering you up and receiving your maternal blessing, if only in letters.

Only a few years ago, when my way led through the northern camps, how much comfort and good cheer your letters full of motherly love brought me! For me, each one was a holiday, full of light!

I preserved your letters carefully and read them through, time and time again, sitting on my plank-bed. My heart was flooded with renewed spiritual power and hope in the Lord!

My mother was placed in Lukyanov prison in Kiev. The fabrication of a criminal case began.

How all this brings to mind the years 1930 to 1937, when a criminal case was made out three times against my father—a Christian, costing him his life. It is true they rehabilitated him posthumously. The atheist authorities were forced to admit his complete innocence. Now, however, his sixty-four-year-old widow has been subjected to incarceration in prison on the same religious grounds.

Great grandmother, Maria (left), Lydia (right), and Georgi Vins' little daughter, Natasha—circa 1960

The conditions of my mother's confinement in prison were appalling. At the trial she said, "Whatever your sentence may be, it will amount to a death sentence because the conditions in which I find myself in my cell are unbearable!"

My mother's trial took place in Kiev on February 8th and 9th 1971. My wife, eldest daughter, and son, and not more than fifteen Christians were present in the court, although about a hundred Christians wanted to be at the trial. The court was small. My mother spoke quietly, calmly, confidently. The prosecutor raised his voice frequently and showed irritation.

Out of the many written petitions signed by my mother and other prisoners' relatives from 1966 to 1970, the investigation selected four facts about persecution for the faith which the court tried to represent as lies and slander. What is more, they did not summon to court as witnesses those who had suffered, but those who directly or indirectly had been guilty of persecution for the faith—workers in the procuracy, militia, and camp administration who, performing their official duty, said what the persecutors wanted them to say.

My mother declared in her defense speech: "How can investigators and militiamen, those very people about whom we are complaining, act as witnesses? Not a single person who has suffered was called as a witness. In this light, the trial begins to look somewhat absurd!"

It is not surprising, therefore, that my mother was sentenced to three years' deprivation of freedom.

Taking account of her arrest and her weak state of health, this was almost a death sentence! But what do they care about that? The atheist judges of the '70s? They are repeating what their predecessors did in the famous year of 1937, through whose hands my father passed to his death.

MY MOTHER'S DEFENSE SPEECH

(Extracts)[5]

February 9th, 1971
Kiev regional court

First, I would like to say that I did not demand any sort of international tribunal, although the Procurator called this raving nonsense, but in actual fact I asked at the beginning of the trial that a Christian lawyer, a representative of international Christian society, might be present, and that he might carry out my defense as a Christian. This was my right.

I consider that the trial has certainly violated judicial procedure as it is apparently called in legal terminology. How can investigators and militiamen, the very people about whom we are complaining, act as witnesses? Not a single person who had suffered was called as a witness. In this light, the trial begins to look somewhat absurd . . .

As Evangelical Christian-Baptists, our creed is such that we respect the authorities. In the Soviet Union, our denomination is permitted because it contains no fanaticism. We always carry out our duties as citizens better than others, and one can say only good about my fellow-believers sitting in this room. For we know that all authority comes from God, but we do not want to disobey Christ's commands: "Go into all the world and preach the gospel," "Give to Caesar what belongs to Caesar, but to God what belongs to God," "Suffer the little children to come unto me," and so on . . .

The church is separated from the state. The church must have one head—Christ, as we understand it, He who came down to Earth and will come a second time . . .

(The judge, interrupting: "Do not digress; keep to the point of the charge.")

We petitioned at first for the release of our relatives but did not touch upon the country's laws; this was the job of the All-Union Council and the Council of Churches. But then we began to investigate what our relatives were being tried for, which led to our investigating the laws. We ascertained that in the first Constitution of the Soviet Union both anti-religious and religious propaganda were allowed. Later religious propaganda was forbidden. Only the words, "Everyone has the right to profess his own religion" were left, and anti-religious propaganda was allowed! But even though only "profess" is left, we still have the right to preach. For the word "profess" means telling others about our faith, and not only performing rites.

At first, from June 1966 onwards, we went in delegations in Moscow to the General Procurator Rudenko, to the Supreme Soviet, to the Central Party Committee and asked them to receive us. We sent telegrams so that they would receive us and hear us out. But they answered—do not come and do not ask anything, it will not help you at all, nobody will listen to you.

(The judge: "But they were sentenced, therefore they were guilty.")

Why did we start to write? Someone was arrested here, then there, and then in many places, and so we began to write our reports. We called our reports "emergency reports." Our council is mainly composed of women—mothers and wives, from all the republics. We could not sit around with our arms folded when our children and our husbands were suffering.

Only four of the facts of which we have written are being investigated here, but we have written about many more. Something of our reports should have been read here. We have written about many deprived of freedom, and their families. In the lists is a column of "dependents." Basically, these are large families, with seven, eight, nine, ten or eleven deprived children, left without a breadwinner.

We wrote that Golev, an old man, was arrested. He is seventy-three years old. He was sentenced to three years, but in all he has already suffered for nineteen years for the sake of God's Word. He organized a mutual aid fund for deprived children, and for this he was sentenced. How could we not write "condemned to physical destruction" when the breadwinner was arrested and a family of many children abandoned?

No one (among the authorities) gave them a thought or troubled about them, and that means they were left to die of starvation.

We wrote that because we opened our flats for prayer meetings, the owners of the flats were beaten and tried. For example, in Kiev, Shelestun was beaten, and we wrote about it. He had a certificate for remission from beatings from a legal commission. Punishment was inflicted on the head by militia who beat him.

We wrote in our reports about the breaking up of prayer meetings with Christians being beaten. Recently, Christians have been seized on the way to a meeting, on railway platforms, at bus-stops; they seized mothers, leaving their little children on the platforms.

We wrote about the Sloboda family from Belorussia. This family came to believe on their own, through radio broadcasts and through reading the Gospel. They stopped drinking and swearing and began to live decent lives. Simply because the mother told her relatives about God, her two children were taken away from her and put in a boarding school, and she was deprived of her freedom for four years. Then they also tore the remaining three small children from their father because he gave them a religious upbringing.

All the facts contained in the reports we gave in our letters were based on documents witnessed by the signatures of victims or of entire local congregations.

We sent our last letter on October 1st, 1970, and I also signed it. In it, we wrote of Iskovsky, an old man from Moscow region who was dying in prison. He had cancer. He did in fact die. An order was issued for his release so he could die at home, but somebody interfered and so he was not released. He died in prison approximately two weeks before my arrest.

We also wrote about those tortured in camps: Khmara from Barnaul, Lanbin from Novosibirsk, Afonin from Moscow region (he had a weak heart and eight children. We asked for his release, but he died in camp) and Kucherenko who died while being interrogated in Nikolaev.

(The judge: "The accused must keep to the point of the charge. Why are you telling us all this?")

But this is the point of my charge. I am charged with writing letters to the government. I want to tell you what I wrote about in them. I wrote about searches, about the confiscation of religious literature, when the Bible, the Gospel, and song books were taken away. Orders for the destruction of this literature have been passed in court.

At the beginning of this movement in 1962, 524 people were arrested, 400 sentenced to fifteen days' imprisonment for taking part in meetings. for worship, which makes 6,000 days in all. Fines of 94,500 rubles in new money were paid for taking part in prayer meetings. Children underwent interrogation.

We wrote our first letter to U Thant at the United Nations in 1967. This was provoked by the fact that our government was taking no measures at all to improve the position of believers. We wrote because we hoped all the same for justice; we believed that at length our government would show humanity. But the procurator has said here that repression will continue.

At this trial, I have heard from the procurator for the first time that the Soviet Union has not signed the Universal Declaration of Human Rights. I shall conclude now. I have nothing against the witnesses. They are in a delicate situation. Who will say that he has beaten somebody? No one, of course. That is all that I wanted to say.

MY MOTHER'S LAST WORDS AT THE TRIAL

My last words will be very brief. I have twice had the opportunity of saying here what I wanted to say. Now I want to ask only one thing: there is a resolution in this case to summon to court all those who signed the letters. I ask that this should not be done. I take everything upon myself.

It was I who took the chief part in this.

Again, I ask the court to take my age and my poor health into account. Whatever your sentence is, it will amount to a death sentence, because the conditions in which I find myself in my cell are unbearable.

That is all that I wanted to say.

After the sentence had been pronounced—three years labor camp, ordinary regime—my wife threw my mother a bouquet of violets. The Christians, mainly young people, began to throw her red carnations.

The prisoner's escort was frightened and began to take the flowers away from her, but she still managed to carry some of them to her cell. When they brought my mother out of the building into the street, where a police car was standing, a large crowd of Christians sang the hymn:

For the faith of the Gospel,
For Christ we shall stand up,
Following His example,
Ever onward, onward after Him.

The battle rages, the flame is hot,
And places shake and sway,
Raise higher the banner
Of Christ the Victor!

After the trial my mother was sent off to a women's camp in Kharkov. Her state of health was grave. She was led off to work supported on people's arms.

A Letter to My Mother

Are you still alive, my old mother?
Behind the high stone wall
The gloomy sentry tramples down
Your gray-haired life, like a toy.

There in prison, as in a den of depravity,
Amid falsehood and human baseness,
You are overcome by deep sorrow
For people enslaved by darkness.

Often you whisper to God in your prayers,
Wilting beside your plank-bed at dead of night:
"Lord! Open to these hearts the way
To everlasting, holy life!"

I know that in your gray-haired years
It is hard to endure prison.
I would give up my life and all my freedom
To replace you, my darling!

1971

Part II: Faithful Servants of God

By Georgi Vins

And they overcame him by the blood of the Lamb, and by the word of their testimony; and they loved not their lives unto the death. (Revelation 12:10-12)

INTRODUCTION

> Moreover it is required in stewards, that a man be found faithful. (1 Corinthians 4:2)

The following pages tell of the life of our brothers and sisters who were faithful to the Lord unto death. The author of these biographical essays, Georgi Vins, the Secretary of the Council of Evangelical Christian-Baptist Churches, was arrested once more in March 1974.

Another servant of the church has joined the several hundred Christians who are in prison in our country, a father of five children, a son who has had no chance of meeting his Christian mother who returned from prison in December 1973.

Only God knows when we shall see our brother and if we shall meet here on Earth. But the poems which he wrote in the difficult moments of his first imprisonment are full of radiant hope for us—

Hoisting the sail of radiant faith,
I shall race to my longed-for homeland,
And look into the eyes of Christ,
Who has stretched out His hands to life!

I shall say with a smile to my dear ones:
"My darlings . . . but tears . . . are not needed!
I shall wait in heaven for you,
The conquerors of death and hell!"

He that overcometh shall inherit all
things; and I will be his God, and he
shall be my son. (Revelation 21:7)

FOREWORD

Man needs Christ. The fishermen of Galilee and the Scythian nomads, the slaves and the free men, the wise and the ignorant of the first century, when the fame of mighty Rome thundered throughout the world, all needed Him. We also need Christ in the twentieth century, the century of atomic energy and space exploration, for only Christ grants real meaning to our present life (John 10:10; 14:6) and an unshakable foundation for our future eternal life, the beginning of which is here on Earth through faith in the Son of God (John 3:36). A boundless and mighty development of all man's spiritual powers is found only in Christ. Christ is the greatest gift from Heaven, its supreme blessing. Preachers of the Gospel bear the news of Christ throughout the world to all peoples.

For over a hundred years, Christians of the Evangelical-Baptist faith in our country have preached Christ amidst persecution to their own people. Suffering abuse and slander, enduring persecution for their faith, they do not grumble and complain of their fate. They give thanks to God for this special love for the Russian people, which gives them immense power to testify to Christ in an atheist environment not only in prayer houses but also in courtrooms, prison cells, and distant camps.

Believers of the Evangelical Christian-Baptist church desire to remain faithful to Christ and in no way to yield to unbelief (2 Peter 1:10; Revelation 21:7).

Not so long ago, many people in our country supposed that there were almost no believers in the Soviet Union.

By the '60s, the voice of the church had become very faint. Witness to Christ was bounded more and more by the walls of prayer houses, but inside these houses, the number of which has catastrophically decreased, ministers who had been false to God under the pressure of atheism led the task of curtailing the whole work of the Gospel.[6]

But here the Lord showed His mercy. It is "time for thee, Lord, to work" as the psalmist said, "for they have made void thy law" (Psalm 119:126).

The Action Group of the Evangelical Christian-Baptists, formed in 1961, appealed to all believers of the Evangelical Christian-Baptist church with a call to revival: to purity, holiness, and faithfulness in serving the Lord.

Atheism threw the entire state machine against the revived fellowship: the press, radio, television, police organs, procurators' offices, law-courts, prisons, labor camps, and the Committee for State Security (the KGB).

However, the Lord gave His church the strength to defend the work of evangelism. Then the whole country began to talk about the might of Christ and the power of His ideas.

Atheists try to distort the essence of Christ's teachings and slander His followers, but the very fact of open, bitter war with God establishes a healthy concept in the consciousness of the Russian people: the matter concerns a living God, for one does not wage war with the dead!

Russia's best people saw the happiness of their own nation only through God. Among these people was Nikolai Odintsov, a martyr for the faith of the Gospel. As long ago as 1927, he wrote in the journal *The Baptist*, No. 1: "I anticipate a great spiritual awakening of my own people, a broad and deep reformation movement in our vast land that is so rich in opportunities."

Thousands of Russia's Christians dying in prisons and camps prayed for this awakening. God's dear servant Ivan Stepanovich Prokhanov prayed for this in his years of exile in a strange land.

The Christian prisoners of the '70s and all our longsuffering Christian-Baptist brotherhood pray for the spiritual awakening of the Russian people and all the peoples of our multinational land.

The following pages contain several short essays on faithful men and women who served God: Nikolai Odintsov, Pavel Ivanov-Klyshnikov, Pavel Datsko, Georgi Shipkov, Alexander Shalashov, Pavel Zakharov and others. They also contain several of their letters, sermons and articles.

I also direct my dear readers' attention to the fundamental principles of the Evangelical Christian-Baptists. They layout the basis of the formation of our brotherhood from the very first days of its origin in 1867.

Fundamental Principles of the Evangelical Christian-Baptists.[7]

◊ The Holy Scripture (the Bible) is the only rule and guidance in all matters and questions of faith and life. It follows from this that the preaching of the Gospel or witnessing to Christ is the chief task and the fundamental mission of the church.

◊ Absolute freedom of conscience.

◊ The church of God consists, exclusively, of regenerate people. (Spiritual regeneration of members.)

◊ Baptism of believers.

◊ The independence of each separate local church.

◊ The priesthood of all believers.

◊ The separation of the church from the State.

Thousands of servants of God in our country worked for these principles, for the purity of Evangelical teaching. Many of them yielded up their lives in prisons and camps, but they did nor betray the teaching of Jesus Christ!

My great desire is to summon my friends in the faith to preserve and increase the precious spiritual heritage of the Evangelical-Baptist brotherhood, to propagate the principles of our doctrine, to know and love the history of on brotherhood.

The letters, sermons, notes, and photographs of the dear and faithful servants who were before us, memories of them, and most of all the spirit of their pure and selfless service—this is our heritage, our spiritual wealth, about which every Christian should know.

May this work serve for the strengthening of the faith and the increase of the number of faithful servants of God in the harvest field of the Gospel!

> Wherefore the rather, brethren, give diligence to make your calling and election sure: for if ye do these things, ye shall never fall. (2 Peter 1:10)

> Jesus saith unto him, I am the way, the truth, and the life: no man cometh unto the Father, but by me. (John 14:6)

NIKOLAI ODINTSOV

> Remember them which have the rule over you, who have spoken unto you the word of God: whose faith follow, considering the end of their conversation. (Hebrews 13:7)

"I anticipate a great spiritual awakening of my own people, a broad and deep reformation movement in our vast land that is so rich in opportunities. I bear the approach of Him who is coming to us from the heavens in the fullness of His glory and with a joyfully beating heart, I turn to Him and pray fervently, 'Come, Lord Jesus!'" Thus wrote Nikolai Odintsov, in the journal *The Baptist*, No. 1, 1927 as he was praying and anticipating a great spiritual awakening in our land.

For many years now, the believers of our brotherhood have remembered Nikolai Odintsov with great warmth, love, and respect. Many who knew him personally bear witness that he was a very modest and simple brother, sympathetic, thoughtful, and attentive to everyone.

His brother ministers emphasize Odintsov's extreme adherence to principle in matters of faith, his faithfulness to Evangelical teaching, his courage and steadfastness in the defense of preaching, and the absence of any inclinations at all to compromise with unbelief.

The Lord placed him to serve in a most responsible post at one of the most difficult periods of the history of our Evangelical-Baptist brotherhood.

Odintsov did not yield, did not retreat, and in no way betrayed the work of God. He remained to the end in the high position of Chairman of the Christian-Baptist Union until the very day of his arrest in 1933 and shared the full burden of persecution for the faith with the entire brotherhood. Nikolai Odintsov died as a martyr for God's cause.

For the generation of young people who came into the church in the war years and in the first years after the war, Nikolai Odintsov and his comrades in the ministry were examples to be imitated.

Years passed by . . . More and more new generations of believers came into the church. For many young Christians, the name Nikolai Odintsov was buried far away in the depths of time.

The leadership of the All-Union Council buried in oblivion the names of faithful servants of God who had died in the camps. And it was forbidden even to pray for those who were still languishing in prison.

In old Christian journals, which have become a great rarity after innumerable arrests and searches, the ministry of Odintsov and other brothers comes to an abrupt end in 1928, and what happened later was passed on only by word of mouth, under one's breath . . .

Nikolai Odintsov

Nikolai Odintsov was born on December 8th, 1870. Three years before his birth, Nikita Isaevich Voronin, the pioneer of the Evangelical-Baptist brotherhood in Russia, turned to the Lord and received the baptism of faith. A living torrent of Evangelical teaching began to flow across the plains of Russia, drawing into its ranks all those who were thirsting for salvation and eternal life.

The news of the Gospel reached Nikolai Odintsov also. He turned to the Lord as a young man of twenty. In Christ, he found salvation and the meaning of life.

In 1891, Odintsov entered into an eternal covenant with the Lord and was baptized. The baptism was performed in the Volga in Saratov district. The heavens and the waters of the Russian river heard his vow to serve the Lord in good conscience. Odintsov kept his vow. He dedicated his whole lift to witnessing to Christ, right up to his martyr's death.

Nikolai Odintsov was the first living stone set by God in the house building of the Saratov Evangelical Christian-Baptist church. It was here also that his preaching ministry began.

In 1909, Odintsov was ordained to the ministry of preaching. He was ordained by brother V. V. Ivanov-Klyshnikov, together with brothers D. I. Mazaev, S. P. Stepanov and V. P. Stepanov. After his ordination, Odintsov visited many communities of our brotherhood. He preached in the towns and villages of Povolzhe and the Caucasus, in Moscow and Petersburg. Everywhere his spiritual labor was accompanied by abundant spiritual blessings from the Lord.

In 1913, he made his first visit to the most distant region of Russia—the Far East. The believers of the Far East were cut off from the whole Evangelical Christian-Baptist brotherhood because of the great distances and the constant shortage of itinerant preachers. Every visit to their region by brothers from central Russia brought them great encouragement and strength in the faith.

After 1917, Nikolai Odintsov took a most active part in the publishing of Christian journals, pamphlets, and books, and was blessed in his work in the Moscow Evangelical Christian-Baptist church.

On December 15th, 1924, the Plenum of the All-Union Council of Baptists took place in Moscow, at which Ilya Andreevich Golyaev was elected chairman of the Council and Odintsov assistant and treasurer. The newly elected Council in the person of its chairman defined its main task thus:

> As I enter into such a responsible position before the Lord, in the strength of our Lord's command: "Go ye into all the world, and preach the gospel to every creature" (Mark 16:15), I set as my chief task, the directing of all my abilities and all our united resources to the work of mission. This was the mandate given to me by the Plenum of the Council of our Fraternal Union in accordance with the will of God.[8]

In January 1925, after a seven-year break, publication of *The Baptist* was renewed, and from the fourth issue, Odintsov was its editor.

In 1926, there began a particularly responsible period in Nikolai Odintsov's life and ministry. At the 26th Baptist Congress in Moscow in 1926, Odintsov was elected Chairman of the Federal Baptist Union. In these years, he was constantly delivering sermons about Christ, lecturing on Bible courses in Moscow, and making trips to conferences and congresses of the vast Evangelical Christian-Baptist brotherhood in our country. He took part in the work of conferences and congresses in Siberia, the Far East, Central Asia, Povolzhe, the Ukraine, and also the fourth World Baptist Congress in Toronto in 1928.

During his visits to Evangelical Christian-Baptist churches in different parts of our country, Odintsov attached great importance to conversations about the basic principles of Evangelical Christians-Baptists.

His aim was that all the brotherhood should have a profound mastery of the basic principles of our doctrine and that they should be widely disseminated; for in these principles is concentrated the fundamental Gospel truth of the apostolic church—the preaching church, the missionary church.

In 1929, the forces of atheism attacked the work of the Gospel in our country.

In the summer of 1929, the journal *The Baptist* was closed down. Only seven issues of the journal came out in 1929. In autumn of the same year, the Bible courses were stopped. Students who had arrived to begin their studies went sadly back home.

On the brink of the impending persecution, Odintsov wrote the article "A Model for the Faithful," which was published in the second issue of *The Baptist* of 1929.

In this article, which was dedicated to the selfless servant of God Vasily Ivanov-Klyshnikov, who remained faithful to God through the persecutions of the Tsarist regime, Odintsov was preparing the Evangelical Christian-Baptist brotherhood for new trials for the faith.

In this article Odintsov wrote:

> Looking to the Author and Finisher of our faith, Ivanov-Klyshnikov always performed the exalted work of a servant of the Lord joyfully and with deep humility, despite the deprivations and trials connected with this work, the defamation and unjust gossip, the constraint and persecution.

More than once he had to convince himself in practice that "we are accounted as sheep for the slaughter" (Romans 8:36), and that "it is given in the behalf of Christ, not only to believe on him, but also to suffer for his sake" (Philippians 1:29); and he was not surprised "concerning the fiery trial . . . as though some strange thing happened" (1 Peter 4:12), remaining unshakable in affliction in the recognition knowing "that we are appointed thereunto" (1 Thessalonians 3:3).

In 1929, Odintsov's closest assistant, the Secretary of the Federal Baptist Union, Pavel Ivanov-Klyshnikov, the son of the above-mentioned Vasily Vasilievich, was arrested and sent off to Kazakhstan.

In the same year, the authorities closed down the Baptist Union itself. It is true that in 1930 this leading Baptist body renewed its activity, but now it was on a federal basis since the authorities had dissolved the local Baptist Unions. Although the Union's fraternal center had resumed its work, it had no printing organ or itinerant preachers.

In May 1930, the secret police confiscated a house in Moscow at 29 Brestskaya Street, which belonged to the Baptist Union. It housed Bible courses, the offices of the Union, and the living quarters of the workers of the Union's administration: Odintsov, Datsko, and Ivanov-Klyshnikov.

All these years Nikolai Odintsov made a courageous stand for the work of God in our land and to the end remained faithful to his calling and his election. He struck no bargains with atheism.

Nikolai Odintsov realized that soon he would face separation from his nearest and dearest, from his friends in the faith and in service. At that time, thousands of brothers were already languishing in exile, in prisons and in camps for the faith of Christ. Odintsov encouraged the believers, calling them to courage and faithfulness to the Lord to the very end. According to the example of the apostle Paul, he would say to his close friends:

> . . . bonds and afflictions abide me. But none of these things move me, neither count I my life dear unto myself, so that I might finish my course with joy, and the ministry, which I have received of the Lord Jesus, to testify the gospel of the grace of God. (Acts 20:23-24)

On the night of November 5th or 6th,1933, Odintsov was arrested and sentenced to three years imprisonment. He served his term in Yaroslavl Prison. Alexandra Mozgova, a co-worker in the Baptist Union office, was arrested at the same time as Odintsov. She too was sentenced to three years in labor camps. Later, she told how she had had crossed paths with Odintsov during the investigation. Odintsov was led into the investigator's office. He was unshaven and his cheeks were sunken. He gave Alexandra Mozgova a friendly look of encouragement and blessed her for the thorny path which lay ahead of her. Odintsov behaved calmly and with assurance, although physically he was very weak indeed. During the investigation itself, he selflessly defended the things of God.

After his trial, Nikolai Odintsov was sent to Yaroslavl Prison, where he was kept for the whole of his term of imprisonment. After he had served his prison sentence, he was sent into exile in Eastern Siberia. He spent his exile in the village of Makovskoye in Krasnoyarsk district. This village is situated on the River Ket in the taiga, seventy kilometers from Yeniseisk. Makovskoye is an ancient Russian settlement which has just observed its three hundred and fiftieth anniversary. Russian Cossack explorers founded it amid the slumbering Siberian forests. For tens of kilometers around, there is not one village, only taiga and more taiga. Makovskoye is the traditional place of exile for religious people of different faiths. Odintsov was held in Makovskoye before the war, and after the war, many believers served their exile here.

In 1937, Odintsov's wife Alexandra Stepanovna came to see him in Makovskoye. When she returned home, she told the believers that Nikolai was very weak physically but courageous in spirit. He sent greetings to his brothers and sisters and was preparing to pass on to the eternal dwelling place of the Father. He often said to his wife, "I want to go home!"

There in Makovakoyc in 1938, Odintsov was once again put under guard and taken away in an unknown direction.

Soon he died in prison.

Nikolai Odintsov's memory lives on among the whole Evangelical Christian-Baptist brotherhood. His selfless, uncompromising service for the work of the Gospel and his faithfulness to Christ until death are an inspiring example for many thousands of Christians.

A LETTER FROM ODINTSOV IN PRISON[9]

(Krasnoyarsk district)

My dear brother in the Lord S.A.!

Peace to you and to all those who love the Lord! All of you are uncertain about me . . .

I shall not describe the terrors which the prisoners are experiencing, as that is a matter for a specialist historian or a simple honest man. I shall say only one thing: there is no terror like it! Can one imagine the bestial look of the handpicked convoy escorts, who, making use of the right granted them, can shoot sick men who collapse and hunt down with vicious dogs the prisoner who falls on the road?

Can one become accustomed to constant, coarse, inhuman shouting flavored with the most awful, infernal swearing which lowers human dignity? Can one endure the constant, daily, tiresome, loathsome activity of the provocateurs and spies, who hang on one's every word and wrench at a prisoner's soul?

My body is tired and weak; my work for the Lord here in the camps is unbearably hard, and the repressions I suffer often hold me for long periods on my bare plank bed, which represents my bed of ease.

My dear brother, you presented a petition for me to be set free ahead of time, for a "pardon," for my return to my family and my brothers in the faith. You know, of course, not as a lawyer but as a preacher in God's harvest field, that I, as the least brother in the Lord, was set free forever and pardoned once and for all.

As far as my return to my family is concerned, I shall await my family and our family up there in Heaven, "where we shall meet you beyond the wonderful river and there with incessant praise, we shall serve Jesus . . ."

I have grown weak in body, but not in spirit. Jesus, my Lord, upholds me. I am informed about you only through hearsay. My body cannot bear the violence . . . "For I am already on the point of being sacrificed; the time of my departure has come." Nothing atheistic has adhered to me. "I have fought the good fight, I have finished the race, I have kept the faith." I have refused to betray God. "Henceforth there is laid up for me a crown of righteousness, which the Lord, the righteous judge, shall give me at that day: and not to me only, but unto all them also that love his appearing" (2 Timothy 4:6-8). I have always avoided every injustice. With this, my earthly life will finish. Amen.

I often think that the brothers and sisters with whom I have shared joy, who were once given as gifts by the Lord God in the name of His Son, our Savior, will never see me again, and I shall not see all of you on this Earth. I feel especially sad for the young people, for the servants of the church, for all my brothers and sisters, for soon the terrors of persecution will fall upon you, and it is possible that members of families will suffer—fathers, mothers, children, and grandchildren, wives and husbands, and sisters and brothers. Abuse of God and slander of the children of God will grow up, and "apostates from the Holy Covenant" will appear. Their perfidiousness, cowardice, and servility to atheism will lead to betrayal and subversive activity in the church of Christ, since both verbally and in writing, they will justify atheist activity directed at the destruction of the church.

With the help of the apostates, atheism will lead its faithful people into bodies for the control of church affairs, which with the help of slander and provocation and the exposure of people not servile to atheism will take its slanderous fabrications to the secret police as denunciations as a result of which many servants of the church—brothers and sisters—will suffer. Atheism will enter into an agreement with the apostates from the Holy Covenant. "And such as do wickedly against the covenant shall he corrupt by flatteries: but the people that do know their God shall be strong, and do exploits" (Daniel 11:32).

The Leninist decree on the separation of the church from the State and of the School from the church on January 23rd, 1918 was the first legislative deed to define the rights of citizens of the USSR with respect to religion. By this decree and by other deeds of law, it is forbidden to publish any other laws or resolutions which could change the Leninist decree of January 23rd, 1918 or could limit or change freedom of conscience in our land.

In his article "Socialism and Religion," Lenin wrote "We require that religion should be a private matter as far as the state is concerned. The state must have nothing to do with religion. Religious societies must not be connected with the state power. Religious and church societies must be completely free unions of like-minded citizens independent of the authorities."

It was a wise decision, judicious in the highest degree, which led to the creation of the Constitution of the RSFSR and its thirteen articles, and also the above-mentioned Decree of the Council of Peoples' Commissars of January 23rd, 1918 "On the separation of the church from the State and of the School from the church," as a result of which genuine freedom of conscience was ensured in the great land of the USSR.

Soon after Lenin's death, to be precise on April 8th, 1929, the Resolution of the All-Union Central Executive Committee and the Council of Peoples' Commissars "On Religious Associations" was published. This Resolution is not the last word in the chain of the infernal scheme of atheism to force the faithful children of the living God to their knees before the god of this world, Baal-atheism.

Many brothers and sisters of different ages, from young men to those advanced in years, are found, and will be found for the time being, in chains for faith in the God who foresees and holds everything in His power, and in Jesus, our Savior.

Pitiless in its senseless cruelty, atheism threw into prisons and camps many, many brothers and sisters who were faithful to their Lord. However, those who are faithful to the Teacher, Jesus our Lord, will go forward and will not stop because the path pointed out by the Savior is the right and sure path, and believers who love their Lord will never stand upon the path of compromise with godless atheism.

There will be apostates from the Holy Covenant. In collaboration with atheists ignorant in spiritual matters, and under their leadership, apostates will attempt to introduce division into the brotherhood. They will support this division in order to justify confidence in themselves and to render what is due in gratitude for a quiet life for the status they have received from atheism. After the apostates will rush those who do not hold truth dear, who will also crave thirstily for status and an easy life, those who, no matter whether afflictions and sufferings increase for their believing fathers and mothers, the members of their family, their nearest and dearest, no matter whether afflictions and sufferings increase for the church of Christ—for the time being, they will go about their treacherous business to please atheism.

This is how the struggle with religion in the USSR will be: in time, it will turn into a shameful business in the eyes of the whole world for the leaders of this struggle, since these savagely cruel people will force the closure of prayer houses on believers and churches, will oppress the servants of the church, and even physically torture and liquidate some brothers. They will construct a "case" as a result of biased investigations based on slander, and believers one and all will be condemned to prisons and camps. "Good publicity" about the unjust trials, the procurators and investigators, the camp and prison administrations will be spread throughout the world. All their actions will win approbation, as will these who pioneer, inspire, and lead the campaign.

The legislator who published the resolution on religious associations was so eager to begin a cruel repression of religion that he did not even see the contradiction between this resolution and Lenin's Decree of 23rd January 1918 and article 13 of the 1918 Constitution. If the Decree and article 13 of the Constitution granted believers a church independent of the state and the freedom to spread their faith, then the resolution had contrary aims: specifically, to put the church in a position of complete dependence on the atheist state, to which would be granted the absolute right of depriving believers of freedom of conscience. In its war with religion, atheism will try to suppress freedom of religion by repression throughout the land.

It is also possible that conditions will be created for the church with the intention of physically annihilating believers. Let us remember the history of martyrdom of the apostolic church of the first centuries, when the most cruel of all the Roman Caesars governed the people: Nero, Decius, Diocletian, and others. Let us remind all our believing brothers and sisters what happened in those centuries under these rulers who were also high priests of the pagan religion which held sway in the Roman Empire. The most cruel persecution of Christians occurred because of the slander of high priests and other priests of paganism.

The rulers of Rome used this persecution to pursue their aim of finally eradicating Christianity, the "sect of Christ," which was hostile to the pagan religion of the Empire.

It was announced that all the Christians in the towns and villages should appear on a stated day and hour in stated places for the offering of pagan sacrifices. They hunted out those who did not appear and applied to them the most refined tortures and slow-acting torments, at the same time forcing the believers to renounce Christ. Those who did not appear were deprived of civil rights, their property was confiscated, and their families were broken up. Christians were crucified on crosses, sewn up in the skins of animals and given like this to wild animals to be torn to pieces. They were sewn up in sacks, which were soaked in tar and set alight during the so-called people's festivals.

Christians were driven out of their homes because they gathered for prayer, but prayer houses were taken away. Christians were whipped, stoned, dragged along the ground, thrown into pits and prisons, deprived of burial, set upon by hungry, vicious, man-eating dogs The bodies of tortured Christians lay in heaps in the streets of the towns.

The Christians of the apostolic church went out to preach the Word of God from the catacombs, hovels, and forests where the true Christians of the apostolic church would gather for prayer and to glorify the Eternal God: their great song of faith, love, and hope has continued through the following ages and will continue to resound. It is a song of praise to the Almighty Lord God, and it speaks of and glorifies God's all-inclusive forgiveness and love to the whole of mankind. It calls man to moral purity and to sanctity. This song is sung by many people on all the continents of Earth in our own times.

Several days ago during a convoy transfer, I, being one of the weakest prisoners, was unable to stand, and at that moment, I heard a shout behind me and the momentary prick of something sharp in my back Then I was thrown to the ground by a blow below my head. The next moment, I heard swearing and felt two vicious dogs on top of me, snarling, trampling over me, and tearing my already torn and dirty clothing. Then I felt a sharp pain below my stomach, where the dog's teeth were tearing to pieces my old, exhausted body which had suffered so much. I came to myself in the barracks, where my comrades, prisoners in the Lord, were binding up my wounds.

Within only three weeks, I was led out and driven on to a convoy for work.

What else will there be? The Lord knows! Eternal glory to Him! Rejoice, dear brothers and sisters, as I rejoice! Your brother to the end of his days has not forgotten you all, and may the name of our God and of His Son our Lord Jesus Christ be blessed and glorified!

Amen, Hallelujah!

PAVEL DATSKO

1884-1941

Jesus, Savior of my soul,
Let me cling to your breast,
Be my protector amid storms,
Do not desert me along the way!
I have no other refuge,
All I have is you alone,
Do not abandon me, weak as I am,
Amid worldly vanity.

How often we have sung this hymn with deep emotion and reverence in the presence of the Savior. This hymn not only calls us to a special intimacy with Christ; it also leads us into the sanctuary of God. This is evident from the radiant faces of those who sing it and those who listen. Who was the author of this remarkable hymn? For many long years, 1 did not know . . . but I felt that he must be a Christian of deep spirituality and marked poetic sensitivity.

Some years ago, the Lord allowed me to learn who the author was. He was Pavel Yakovlevich Datsko.

Believers who knew him personally have the most joyful memories of him as a simple, sensitive Christian whose spirit never failed.

Pavel Datsko, a gifted preacher and a poet who drew his inspiration from above, was respected and loved by all our brotherhood, especially in the Ukraine where he labored so hard in the harvest-fields of God.

Datsko was the author of many remarkable Christian poems, some of which have become hymns—"Jesus, Savior of my Soul," the Christmas carol "The Angels' Song," "Thou art my Savior" and others.

His poems were frequently printed in the journals *The Baptist* and *The Ukrainian Baptist*, but some were never published, including the long poem "Ruth."

Pavel Datsko was born on 28th August 1884 in the Ukraine, where the greater part of his life and his spiritual ministry were spent.

In May 1925, there took place in Kharkov the fourth congress of Baptists of the Ukraine, at which the All-Ukrainian Baptist Union was formed. A. P. Kostyukov was elected as chairman and Pavel Datsko as his deputy.

The position of the work of God in the Ukraine at the time of this congress was set forth in the following resolution:

> Congress finds that the Baptist communities of the Ukraine are in a satisfactory condition. It has observed a numerical growth in membership, recently reaching an average of 15 per cent per annum. (*The Baptist,* No. 4-5, pp. 2-3, 1925.)

The Congress defined the main task of the Baptist Union of the Ukraine:

> Missionary activity, that is, the sending of evangelists to spread the Gospel, must be considered to be of the first importance. All other forms of Christian activity must be subordinated to it, and all our attention must be concentrated on it.

In 1926, the 26th congress of Christians-Baptists took place in Moscow, where Pavel Datsko was elected to the governing body of the Federal Baptist Union.

In 1927, he moved from Kharkov to Moscow, where he held the offices of treasurer and deputy chairman of the Union, taught on Bible courses, and worked as one of the editors of *The Baptist.*

Datako never failed to give support to brother Odintsov in his work, especially in the difficult period of harassment and persecution which began in 1929.

In 1928, Pavel Datsko dedicated the following poem to Nikolai Odintsov on his birthday:

To Nikolai Odintsov

Days of bygone feelings,
Expectations,
Hesitations,
Have flown away like a dream.
They have passed,
Hidden in the distance,
Only their memory is clear.

A new time has come,
Heavenly labor,
And severe,
Promises fruit of peace,
Weariness,

Consolation,
Fill all the present year.

Now the time of days to come;
Which make all things possible,
Which bring once more
Blessing upon blessing.
Without doubt
Or confusion,
Brother, you must face them.

In 1929, brother Pavel Ivanov-Klyshnikov (from page 107) was sent into exile, and all the work of the executive secretary of the Baptist Union now fell on Pavel Datsko's shoulders.

In 1933, Odintsov was arrested. Pavel Datsko was the only one left of the older, experienced members of the leadership of the Baptist Union. In 1936, he too was sent into exile, from which he did not return until the autumn of 1938. His wife, Vera Ivanovna, lived at this time in the town of Berdyansk in the Ukraine. Pavel Datsko was free for less than a year. He was arrested in Berdyansk in March 1939 and sentenced to ten years in labor camp without right of correspondence. He died in a camp in Siberia in 1941. His wife died a lonely old woman in Moscow in 1967.

In 1938, after his exile and not long before his arrest, Pavel Datsko said, "I want to write the history of the Evangelical Christians-Baptists in Russia from their very beginning." However, he was not destined to write the history of our brotherhood. But his literary legacy, his name, and his whole life have passed irrevocably into the history of our brotherhood as one of the true and courageous servants of the Gospel, a talented poet, and a martyr for God's cause.

> [T]hey shall be mine, saith the Lord of hosts . . . and I will spare them, as a man spareth his own son that

> serveth him. Then shall ye return, and discern between the righteous and the wicked, between him that serveth God and him that serveth him not. (Malachi 3:17-18)

Our Evangelical brotherhood sings Datsko's hymns, and amid severe trials is making its way toward that Heavenly country of which he wrote so movingly:

O my beautiful homeland,
The goal to which I yearn!
Each hour my song
Rings out to you from here.

A stranger here—my home is there;
For there is no chain
That can fetter my free spirit
Outside my homeland.

In my native land on earth
My life is a burning flame,
I cannot number here
The friends that God has given.

Yet still I strive towards heaven
Through the burning heat of the journey;
I am there in spirit,
I yearn to enter there.

Although my path is narrow
And the thorny way is grim,
Strength is abundant
Amid the mountain of holy gifts.

My staff is God's word;
His spirit is my treasure;
Only there in the land of consolation
Will I lay down my head to rest.

O, who will go there with me
To that beautiful Canaan,
There is perfect rest for toil,
Long ago I was called there.

Let us all go, all who suffer here,
For whom this world is strange,
Only there will you all find rest,
In the land that is my home!

PAVEL IVANOV-KLYSHNIKOV

1886-1941

On 25th June 1928 at the Fourth World Baptist Congress in Toronto, Canada, Pavel Vasilievich Ivanov-Klyshnikov, the Secretary of the Federal Baptist Union, delivered an address titled, "The work and tasks of Baptists in the USSR."

> Among all the so-called sectarian currents in Russia, the Baptists were the most significant current as regards the number of followers, the strictest in defense of the purity of their doctrine, the most steadfast in the terrible persecutions of the Tsarist epoch, and the most strikingly ardent as regards the missionary spirit that burned within them!
>
> We have no precise statistics. We have approximately 200 thousand baptized members . . .

It is clear from this that evangelization has barely touched the Russian people. In many places, people have never even heard the preaching of the Gospel . . .

For 4,000 communities and groups, we have about 900 pastors, and 3,100 communities and groups are left without trained leaders. For 5,000 local churches, we own only about 400 prayer-houses, and we have about 800 rented ones, but the other 3,800 churches are in private homes.

Our work in the USSR is still in this embryonic state. Nevertheless, the Russian people are exceptional in the depth of their religious feelings and their religious quest. It is the most fruitful spiritual soil among all the peoples of the Earth. It is a God-seeking people, a God-bearing people, in the words of the famous Russian philosopher Vladimir Solovyov . . .

Side by side with this task of evangelization we are faced by no less a task within our communities, educational work . . .

. . . What I wanted to emphasize especially was this, that the evangelization of our land has a world-wide significance in the development of God's work on earth.

Russia is not Europe, but she is not Asia either: she is a mediator between two worlds. And the light of Christ which will flare up in her will light and warm both the West and the East!"(*The Baptist*, 1928, No. 7, pp. 4-5.)

The seven thousand participants of the World Congress listened with great attention to Pavel Ivanov-Klyshnikov's speech since he was speaking in the name of the Russian brotherhood, which had preserved its faithfulness to God at the time of the most cruel persecutions under the Tsarist regime, and has raised high the banner of evangelization after 1917. Pavel Ivanov-Klyshnikov himself came from a long line of Russian Protestants.

It will not be without interest to acquaint the reader with certain facts from the life and work of his father, one of the pioneers of the Russian Evangelical-Baptist movement, Vasily Vasilievich Ivanov-Klyshnikov.

Vasily Ivanov-Klyshnikov came from a Molokan[10] family. From his early years he was distinguished by a zealous quest for God's truth. In 1870, he got to know the small ECB church in Tiflis, which numbered ten members at that time and decided to receive baptism by immersion according to the Word of God. However, when he was interviewed, the believers of the church refused him baptism, pointing to the necessity for belief in the forgiveness of sins and to a personal spiritual communion with God.

Vasily Ivanov-Klyshnikov began to study God's Word sincerely with profound meditation and prayer.

A year later, in 1871, the Tiflis church again put him seriously to the test. Convinced of his regeneration, they admitted him to baptism by immersion. The baptism was performed by N. I. Voronin. From that day, Vasily Ivanov-Klyshnikov began to labor in God's harvest-field. Thanks to his prayers and his witness to Christ in the village of Novo-Ivanovka (in the Transcaucasus), there was formed the second (at that time) Evangelical Christian-Baptist Church in our land after the one at Tiflis.

Vasily Ivanov-Klyshnikov visited hundreds of towns and villages, preaching Christ crucified. For his zealous evangelistic labors, he was subjected to persecution from the authorities of that time.

For about ten years, Ivanov-Klyshnikov was forced into an illegal position while he continued to perform his work in God's harvest-field. From 1890, he contributed to the Evangelical Christian-Baptist journal *Discussion*, which was published secretly. He took a fervent and active part in many congresses of our brotherhood beginning with the first in 1879 in Tiflis.

In 1895, Vasily Ivanov-Klyshnikov was arrested in Baku as a very dangerous criminal and was sent off into exile in the town of Slutsk for five years. He passed in shackles along many kilometers of the prisoner's road, through prisons in Tiflis, Novorossiisk, Feodosiya, Kiev, Kovelya, and Warsaw.

After serving his term of exile, he worked for long years among the believers of the Transcaucasus.

On February 10, 1919, Vasily Ivanov-Klyshnikov passed away. He said to his son Pavel, "I am going home!"

Pavel Ivanov-Klyshnikov turned out to be a worthy successor of his father in the preaching of the Gospel to the Russian people. Thoroughly well-educated and talented, and with a fervent love for the Lord, he contributed with much blessing to our Christian press, and especially to the journal *The Baptist*, where dozens of his articles were published. Among them is an outstanding article about Valtasar Gubmaier, a courageous and faithful preacher of the Gospel in the sixteenth century, who was burnt at the stake in 1528 in Vienna. (*The Baptist*, No 3, 1928.)

In his articles, Ivanov-Klyshnikov called our Evangelical brotherhood to follow courageously after Christ and to witness widely to Him, and not only among the Slavonic peoples. In January 1926 in the article "Tasks of Baptists in the USSR for 1926" (*The Baptist*, Nos. 1-2, 1926), he wrote:

> As always, most attention will be paid to the preaching of the Gospel. In 1926, the work of evangelization will

go in the same direction as in 1925, embracing more and more new places. More attention than formerly will be paid to preaching among Christians of other nations —Armenians, Georgians, Ossetians, and others. In 1926, we intend to promote with particular force the slogan: "Christ for the pagans and Muslims living in the USSR." There are about three million pagans and half-pagans in our land: Kalmyks, Buryats, Chuvash, Chermisy, Mordvinians, Zyryans, Votyaks, Permyaks, Chukchi, Eskimos, and others. They are scattered in the Volga regions and in Siberia. There are about fourteen million Muslims in the USSR: Tatars, Kirgizians, Bashkirs, Nogaitsy, Lezghins, and others.

Valtasar (Baltasar) Gubmaier—1480-1528)

The foundations of missionary work among both the pagans and the Muslims have already been laid down for us. But still it all lies before us. The image of the Macedonian stands persistently before us with the words: "Come and help us."

Now, in-the 'seventies, hundreds of believers in Komi (Zyryans), the Chuvash, the Mordvinians, the Mariitsy, the Udmurts, and other small peoples in our land pray to Christ in their native languages. This is God's answer to the prayers and the selfless labor of the Russian Evangelical Christian-Baptist brotherhood.

In 1926, the 26th congress of Christians-Baptists took place in Moscow, and Pavel Ivanov-Klyshnikov was elected Secretary of the Federal Union of Baptists. The next three years were the most blessed and fruitful of his life and work.

In 1925, he took an active part in the organization of preachers' Bible courses. (They were opened with God's help in 1927 in Moscow.)

In May 1928, he participated in the work of the Fifth All-Ukrainian Congress of Baptists in Kharkov, where be delivered a report on the Bible courses. The Congress of Ukrainian Baptists were filled with deep gratitude to the Lord for the work of the courses and expressed their thankfulness to all the lecturers on the course in the person of Ivanov-Klyshnikov.

Pavel Ivanov-Klyshnikov

In June 1928, he took part in the Fourth World Baptist

Congress, where he was elected to the Executive Committee of the World Baptist Congress. But in 1929, a new period of persecution in our land was already imminent. Pavel Ivanov-Klyshnikov underwent three years of exile in Kazakhstan.

After he had finished his term of exile, he was arrested again in October 1932 and sentenced to ten years in camp.

Until 1937, Ivanov-Klyshnikov's family had periodic meetings with him in the camp and kept up correspondence. But from 1937, the meetings and correspondence stopped abruptly. He never did return home to his family but died in the camp in 1941. For many long years, his family did not know whether he was alive or dead.

Along with Pavel Ivanov-Klyshnikov, his wife Anna went through great trials. In 1941, she was arrested as a Christian and as the wife of a servant of the Gospel; she spent eleven years in prison. Six children were left without a father or mother. But the Lord did not abandon them. Two of them were sheltered during the war in the house of a believing sister, Alexandra Semirech, who lived in Omsk and did much good for the families of Christian prisoners.

Anna Ivanov-Klyshnikov returned from prison in 1952. Soon after her release, she went to the Lord.

The Evangelical Christian-Baptist brotherhood holds Pavel Ivanov-Klyshnikov in remembrance. He remained faithful to the Lord to the end and died a martyr's death for the work of God in our land.

The Evangelical Christian-Baptist brotherhood does not know where Ivanov-Klyshnikov's grave is, nor does it know the date of his death. But the work of God to which he dedicated his life has not died or come to a halt. The church of Christ lives and will continue to live and bear witness of salvation to a perishing world until the day of its rapture for the Lord said,

"I will build my church; and the gates of hell shall not prevail against it" (Matthew 16:18).

A LETTER FROM PRISON

14th May 1933
My dear, beloved wife and darling children: Irusenka, Alyosha, Kolya, Seryozha, Anya, and Vasya.

I expect that tomorrow or the day after I will have a meeting with you. But you can't say everything during a prison meeting, so I am writing to you to supplement what I will tell you at our meeting.

During seven and a half months of separation, I have longed for you with all my heart. For days on end, looking through the barred window to the scrap of blue sky and the peak of the mountain chain in the east, I think of you, and the hand of Almighty God keeps you and me.

The investigation has finished, and since I have committed no crime before the government, it is quite possible that I will be with you somewhere in a new place. May the Lord send us that joy!

But we disciples and fellow-workers of the Lord Jesus Christ must be prepared for people who hate us without cause to treat us severely. Therefore, we will also be ready for a long separation. I am full of joy now when I think that the time will come when we will be inseparable forever. That will be at the end of our earthly life when we will meet again after a temporary separation in the wonderful Kingdom of our Lord.

Now, admitting the possibility of a long separation, I want to bless you each individually.

My dear wife Anna!
I bless you as the co-inheritor of abundant life, as my fellow-laborer in the work of God and as the mother and teacher of our children. Together, we carry the cross of Christ, and together we will rejoice before His Face, but He will give us the happiness of work together in His harvest-field for many years yet. And then He will take us, sated with length of days to His dwelling-place, having let us see our children entering our blessed work!

Dear Irusenka!
I bless you, my beloved daughter! In the early morning of your life, you have stood face to face with need and sorrow and your child's shoulders are bent under the weight of the cross. But the Lord has given you the energy and courage of your mother and the endurance of your father. He has prepared happiness for you on Earth and bliss in eternity. Therefore, do not despair, but on the contrary, rejoice!

My dear, beloved Alyosha!
I bless you as my eldest son. Your child's eyes have already gazed into the black abyss of suffering since armed men took your father from you. But God sees your tender heart and knows how you are able to love warmly and suffer deeply. He has prepared consolation for you in the love of God and men. You will find your happiness in work together with those near and dear to you.

My dear, good Kolya!
The Lord has endowed you with strength and together with your brothers and sisters has appointed you to great service in Christ's work. I want to supplement God's blessings to you with my fatherly blessings. Be happy, my son, and always watch that you do not offend your brothers and sisters in any way. Treat Alyosha especially with full respect as the eldest brother and my deputy; always consult with him about everything.

My dear, darling Seryozha!
Through my prayers and those of your mother, the Lord has preserved your life which has already been exposed several times to serious danger, and in 1927, he clearly showed me that He would heal you of illness. Your development is hampered due to the illnesses you have endured, but the Lord has appointed you to give glory to His name. He has endowed you richly. I give you my blessing to praise the Lord with that poetic and artistic gift and to be happy among those near and dear to you.

My dear little daughter Anya!
You are a living reminder of our banishment for the name of Jesus. You will be our consolation in old age. You pass calmly and safely through every storm and tempest because God has given you the gifts of fearlessness and trust in Him. I bless you, my dear daughter, to pass through life happy and self-sacrificing in the name of God.

My darling, dear Vasya!
The sky above you will not be covered with clouds. With a clear brow, you will offer up prayers to God and they will always be heard. Your birth almost entailed the death of your mother—remember that and love your mother especially.

I give you my blessing to fulfill your service in life for the Kingdom after the example of your grandfather Vasily.

Children, love your mother very much and obey her instructions without any criticism because she bears great difficulties both for you and for me. And among yourselves, love Irusenka and Alyosha above all.

My darling wife! At our meeting, I was infinitely consoled and encouraged by you: you were as bright and cheerful as the spring sun. That is everything. I kiss you warmly, my beloved.—Pavel.

Dedicated to My Wife, Anna Petrovna Ivanova-Klyshnikova, Nee Stryukova

The fulfillment of my youthful fancies,
The embodiment of past dreams,
The blessing of the Almighty,
And my delight—is you!

You had no time to peer at life
With your pure heart and penetrating gaze
Before I came, both close to you and remote,
And together we set out on our journey.

For you and I, my dear, this path
Is a path of spiritual triumphs and victories,
And it leads us to a wonderful land
Where an unfading light shines.

Inspired by our common aspiration
You helped me in my labors,

A sensitive guardian of the purity of convictions,
Of the loftiness of sacred ideals.

It was a joy for me to be with you,
My faithful friend, my dear wife . . .
The prison door has closed behind me,
You are left alone with the children.

You languish in separation, my love,
You tremble like a sensitive doe;
That is a concession to a suffering heart,
An involuntary tribute to the nerves.

You have spent many dragging, cheerless days
And nights of sleeplessness,
You have shed many unconsoled, scalding tears
In the silence of the night.

You had to work painfully
To obtain daily bread for the children;
You have fought like a lioness for the children,
You have suffered like a mother for me.

Your cup of suffering is full,
The way of struggle is everlastingly long.
But the higher the wave of trials,
The fuller the torrent of grace.

The sun of eternal love in the glorious distance
Has continued to shine for you;
Every day on the tablets of your heart
You can write "Ebenezer"![11]

ANNA PETROVNA'S LETTER TO PAVEL IVANOV-KLYSHNIKOV

The following letter was not sent. Anna Petrovna wrote it five years after her husband's death; obviously she had no idea that be had died. [Translator's note.]

My dear, never-to-be-forgotten husband, Pavel!

Today, on your birthday, I congratulate you in my thoughts with all my heart, and from the bottom of my soul, I wish you steadfast faith, hope, strength, endurance, and joy.

I would so much like to be with you on this day, to embrace you, console and caress you, to tell you all about those you love, and who is still alive: our children and I remember you all the time and send our loving and affectionate greeting.

It is the fourteenth year since you were deprived of freedom, the ninth that you have lived without right of correspondence. What have you thought, what have you suffered in that time? Almighty God knows that, and so do you.

Toward the end of the fifth year that I languished in captivity, I had to suffer painfully in prison. Your sufferings now are so close, so familiar to me, and how plain and clear to me it is what you have endured all these years.

You left me young, in the flower of youth and strength, and now I am different. You left your six children as babies, and now they are not so. And if you are foreordained by the Creator to return to us, you will not recognize us.

But I know that you love us more strongly than before, and when we meet, you will embrace us with joyfulness and tender caresses.

All this time I have lived as your widow and have kept totally faithful to you. But time and distance have forced me to grow accustomed to the idea that you are not with us.

Now I do not weep bitter tears over you, and I do not grieve as I did before. For many years now I have waited for you. But I know that we shall meet beyond the grave, where there is no sadness, grief and separation, where joy, happiness and rest await us.

I know that I did not meet you on Earth by chance, but the Lord Himself united us with the bonds of love and marriage, and appointed us a hard path according to our strength. I am grateful to the Lord for our life together with you, for all the sufferings and for His love and mercy to us. How many times in my life I have been near to death, but He protected me and kept me for this life. So how can I be ungrateful or offended by the Creator? Does not the Creator have power over the created? Is it not happiness to be His creature?

It is now the fiftieth year of my life. My dear Pavel, today in a bygone year, your sixtieth year passed away. How few bright days have you seen in the years you have lived? First childhood—full of anxiety and worry because of your father, who was hunted and persecuted by the police. He was the first Baptist in Russia, and for that, he endured exiles and dozens of prisons.

Then long study while in need, living on brass farthings, then strenuous work for a morsel of daily bread, worry about a large, needy family. And life in recent years—one continuous torment.

Now, my friend, I want to tell you about our dear children.

Your eldest daughter, Irina is clever, good, and just. From her very cradle until now she is quiet, modest, and obedient in her own family she has always behaved selflessly, and although there were no conditions for study (she had to give up studying twice), she finished medical institute one of the best students, with excellent marks.

Your three sons, Alyosha, Kolya and Seryozha are tall, fine boys, and all of them look like you.

And our babies are growing up and studying. A year ago, they gave themselves to the Lord and were baptized, which illuminated my life with rays of joy and happiness.

I am happier than you, my friend—I know all about our children! May the Lord bless you in your walk before Him, and may He send you on your journey the pillar of smoke and the pillar of fire so you may reach the eternal Homeland, the radiant holy Homeland, and attain the glorious crown on your head, and be clothed in a white robe.

15th November 1946

I have given them thy word; and the world hath hated them, because they are not of the world, even as I am not of the world. (John 17:14)

GEORGI SHIPKOV

Georgi Ivanovich Shipkov was called to be the exegete of our brotherhood. His spiritual articles were printed in many Evangelical Christian-Baptist journals. They were written in beautiful literary language and with deep reverence for the Person of the Savior. Even today, for the Russian brotherhood, they are a model of profound Russian thought in the study of the Book of Books.

In the journal *The Baptist*, No. 1, 1927, was printed Georgi Shipkov's biography, written by Pavel Ivanov-Klyshnikov. I quote it here with a small abbreviation:

> Georgi Ivanovich Shipkov was born on October 25th, 1865, near Samara. His father was a peasant, a member of the Molokan sect. Georgi received a strict religious education in his family. In 1878, the Shipkovs moved to Blagoveshchensk. Georgi, by then a young man, showed an intense love for reading and the study of languages. Having passed the examination for several classes of high school as an external student, he entered a postal-telegraph office as a clerk and continued studying languages and reading, being chiefly interested in history and philosophy.

> In 1889, Georgi Shipkov turned to the Lord. From that time, he began to be interested in literature on theological questions and read all the books in this field which could be obtained in Blagoveshchenk, in English, French, and German as well as Russian. In order to obtain a systematic theological education, in 1894, Shipkov entered the theological faculty of the American University in Peking where he received the degree of Doctor of Theology in 1898 and immediately returned to Blagoveshehenak. Here he went to work at the telegraph office once more and served there until 1921. As well as this, he was for eight years a lecturer in English in a technical high school and a polytechnic. This work earned brother Georgi the means to live, and at the same time, he undertook spiritual ministry; for about thirteen years, he was deputy pastor of the Blagoveshchensk Baptist community; for seven years, he was a teacher there; for six years, he was Chairman of the Far East Branch of the All-Russian Baptist Union; and for six years, Comrade Chairman of this Branch, which was subsequently re-named the Far East Baptist Union.

In 1928, Georgi Shipkov, as the delegate of the Far East brotherhood, took part in the work of the Fourth Baptist Congress in Toronto.

Shipkov lived almost all his life in Blagoveshchensk and worked zealously for about fifty years in the local church, which was the mother of all the communities of the Far East Evangelical Christian-Baptist brotherhood.

In 1930, as a consequence of the arrest of my father, Peter Vins, who served as pastor of the Blagoveshchensk church from 1927-1930, Georgi Shipkov once more took upon himself a responsible ministry as pastor, which lasted until 1937.

These years were especially hard for our whole brotherhood. The prayer-house in Blagoveshchensk, built by the believers' own hands as long ago as 1910, was confiscated in 1930, and many preachers of the Gospel were forced into exile or were locked up in prisons. Georgi Shipkov was almost the only one left of the ministers of the church in Blagoveshchensk.

Under the influence of persecution in these years, there began to appear among the believers those who were fainthearted, fearful, and even time servers. Fallen and broken officers of the church emerged, and it was from these that the authorities began in subsequent years to form religious groupings obedient to atheism.

The majority of believers, however, courageously continued to serve God.

In 1938, Georgi Shipkov was sent to Omsk. He settled down in a small room in a house belonging to believers. He was physically

Georgi Shipkov (1865-1939)

very weak. But the secret police did not leave him in peace: they often summoned him to interrogations and threatened him with a new exile even farther to the north, in the tundra.

I saw Georgi Shipkov once in Omsk in 1939. He was a short, thin old man with a pointed beard, very affectionate and kind, who laid his small hand on my head and asked about my father.

In the last years of his life (1934-1939), Georgi Shipkov did a great deal of work on the interpretation of the New Testament. His work was contained in a large manuscript book. Unfortunately, the fate of this material is unknown. Perhaps it is intact and is lying around somewhere unused? Perhaps believers are preserving letters, articles, and other manuscript legacies of dear Georgi Shipkov? I beg the Lord to rouse the hearts of believers to seek out the precious spiritual heritage of our heroes of the faith so that it may become the property of our whole Evangelical-Baptist brotherhood.

As an aged man, committed to the Lord to the end, Shipkov ended his earthly journey in prison.

From 1934-1935, there was a lively correspondence between my father and Georgi Shipkov. Unfortunately, only a small number of Shipkov's letters have been preserved. Four of his letters are included in the present collection: a letter to my father from the Blagoveshchensk church (written by Shipkov at the commission of the church), and three personal letters from Shipkov (only a small part of the third letter has been preserved).

LETTERS

Blagoveshchensk to Peter Yakovlevich (Vins)
January 7th, 1934

My greatly respected and warmly beloved brother in the Lord, Peter Yakovlevich, peace to you!

We listened to your letter of December 6th, 1933 to our community at our members' meeting on January 1st, 1934. By this letter, we express to you our most lively gratitude for remembering us and for your exhortations. We have always prayed and will continue to pray for you, that the God and Father of our Lord Jesus Christ will grant you the power of endurance to bear to the end the cross of affliction laid on you, together with the bitterness of separation and the many deprivations on the path trodden by Christ, the apostles, and the martyrs. This is the path trodden by our Savior and Lord and marked out by Him for His followers for all ages (John 15:18-20; Acts 14:22; 2 Timothy 3:12). "Knowing that tribulation worketh patience; And patience, experience; and experience, hope" (Romans 5:3-4). The righteous man and witness of God in the Old Testament, tried and tested by afflictions, clothed in patience, enriched by experience, and inspired with hope, after a whole series of perplexities regarding the way of the Lord, finally says to the Lord: "O Lord, I know that the way of man is not in himself: it is not in man that walketh to direct his steps" (Jeremiah 10:23). In even more ancient, pre-covenant times something similar happened. with another righteous man and sufferer for the Lord, who at the end of a very long series of questions to the air with allusions to the imaginary injustice of God, bordering on open grumbling, finally said to God: "I know that thou canst do every thing, and that no thought can be withholden from thee. Who is he that hideth counsel without knowledge? therefore have I uttered that I understood not . . . Hear, I beseech thee, and I will speak: I will demand of thee, and declare thou unto me. I have heard of thee by the hearing of the ear: but now mine eye seeth thee. Wherefore I abhor myself, and repent in dust and ashes" (Job 42:1-6).

> Be ye also patient; stablish your hearts: for the coming of the Lord draweth nigh. . . .Take, my brethren, the prophets, who have spoken in the name of the Lord,

> for an example of suffering affliction, and of patience. Behold, we count them happy which endure. Ye have heard of the patience of Job, and have seen the end of the Lord; that the Lord is very pitiful, and of tender mercy. (James 5:8-11)

You, my dear and much-beloved brother, write: "Although materially, we sometimes feel need, we are cheerful in spirit and thank the Lord for everything."

We rejoice heartily at this spiritual cheerfulness and sincerely share your grief on account of material need. "Rejoice evermore, pray without ceasing. In everything give thanks" (1 Thessalonians 5:16-18)—such is the threefold principle of Christians in your position.

> Praise Christ, brother for our joy!
> Praise Christ, brother, for the cup of suffering!
> The King of Heaven Himself is coming to us
> And He is bringing us bliss.
> For eternity is already quite near!
>
> (Hymns of Faith, 63)

For each of us, however, who is not in your position, there is another urgent, unremitting principle: "Let him that is taught in the word communicate unto him that teacheth in all good things" (Galatians 6:6), and we have taken it into our heads to put it into practice, although not to the measure we would wish, but to the measure that is possible for us—the minimum. If we have (apparently) not thought about this earlier, then it was as a consequence of a question that troubled us: should our meetings take place in the co-operative-association house or will we, according to the example of the Molokans, have to close them because of the absence of resources to pay for the premises (165 rubles a month, not counting other expenses relating to the maintenance of the building, such as heating, lighting, its protection, and so on)? You can easily imagine what would happen to us, as an organizational unit which for the second winter now has in its care children abandoned at the will of fate by their fathers, if we, as a community, closed down our meetings and thus disbanded ourselves as an organization! Who then would take upon himself the task of going around the homes of the brethren and arousing the former members of the body which had ceased to exist (the community) to do something in the direction alluded to? Every brother and every sister would be morally obliged to do this, but moral obligation is still not practical fulfillment of the obligation, which is entirely dependent upon objective physical reasons and the pressures of everyday life. In general, one may say: if we abandoned our meetings, then our community would lose its identity and disperse. But "having therefore obtained help of God" (Acts 26:22), we stand firm to this day, witnessing with conviction to the truth and openly preaching Christ in our meetings. The help from God consisted of this, that He instilled into us an awareness of the danger that threatened us—to scatter to our homes—and the intention of upholding His work at any price. For the latter, it was necessary for us to make desperate efforts to gather material resources, and only thanks to the voluntary and generous response of members of the community (though not all of them), did we emerge from this tight corner. "I thank Christ Jesus our Lord, who hath enabled me" (1 Timothy 1:12). In the future, we are faced in this respect with the prospect of walking along the path of our creed by forced marches as it is called in military terms. We profoundly believe and entirely hope that He who gave us power in the past until this day will also give it to us in the future, for He is "the same yesterday, and to day, and for ever." (Hebrews 13:8).

Today, we are celebrating a double festival: the day of the resurrection from the dead of our Lord Jesus Christ and the day of His birth into the world (so this is our second Christmas). We are sending to you the material fruit of our meeting today. Accept it as an expression of our powerful love to you.

In conclusion, from my heart I wish you, as I wish myself, a joyful meeting and that you may stay together without parting for an instant in the coming year. I pray to the all-merciful God for this, and I greet you in absence, dear brother Peter Yakovlevich and esteemed sister Lydia Mikhailovna. We remain unfailingly loving you in Christ Jesus, your brothers and sisters in faith, hope and love members of the Blagoveshchensk Baptist community.

For the community and by its commission: G. Shipkov *I, the writer of this letter, greet you in the Lord* (Romans 16:22).

First Letter

Blagoveshchensk
102 Oktyabrskaya Street
February 10th, 1934
Dear and esteemed Peter Yakovlevich!

I was very glad to receive your postcard from Novosibirsk dated January 17th this year, which M. A. Zharikova passed on to me on the 6th of this month at an evening meeting. When I had read the postcard, I also read it at the conclusion of the meeting to those who were with me that evening. Everyone rejoiced and gave thanks to Him who made it possible for you to receive a passport and move to a flourishing town in Siberia from unprepossessing Biisk. We also rejoiced because M A. informed us that the same day she had received a telegram from Lydia Mikhailovna about her move to Novosibirsk. From your postcard and Lydia Mikhailovna's telegram, we concluded that you have managed to find work in your new place. From the bottom of our hearts, we wish you success in your new home and at your new work. We hope that your outward situation will improve gradually, and as for your inward state, we can only rejoice and thank Him who has given us strength.

Doubtless Lydia Mikhailovna has told you about our life, but not everything. After she had left for Biisk, our co-tenants of the co-operative association house were thrown out—and now we are left alone in the building and pay its rent in full (160 rubles a month), as was provided in the contract. Moreover, this winter we have been extremely harassed by lack of fuel, in spite of the legacy and consequences of the reconstruction which has taken place in past years. We have to worry about all this and exert every effort, since at the beginning of autumn, Hamlet's question stood before us: "To be or not to be?" But thanks be to Him who gave us strength: we are! We hope that in the future also we shall be, and, as you know, hope does not disappoint us. However, our co-tenants in the building have condemned themselves to sitting quietly at home.

As a matter of interest, where has V. P. Stepanov gone? V. N. Pertsev has gone on the advice of his doctors to Kislovodsk for treatment for aneurysm (dilation of the heart) and after his return from there, he stopped in Omsk. At present, he is in Khabarovsk. We still don't know what his state of health is.

In conclusion, I send you and our esteemed Lydia Mikhailovna . . . from myself and those who are with me a greeting of love and respect.

A. F. and A. S. Zhbanov are in Omsk at the moment, since their passports have been taken away.

Your sincerely loving,

G. Shipkov.

Second Letter

Blagoveshchensk
102 Oktyabraskaya Street
June 15th, 1935

Dear and greatly respected Peter Yakovlevich, peace to you!

Your kind letter of May 20th, 1935 reached me in good time some while ago. I am very grateful to you for remembering me, for paying attention to me and for your correspondence with me.

From the 12th of May, having rented from one of our members half a house not far from Amur and Zeya for the summer season, we have begun to meet in it twice on Sundays and in the evenings of free days. I shall not say how long I had to petition the local authorities for their permission to hold meetings somewhere in the town.

How dear to me is communion
With the saints on Earth.
But even this delight
Has become impossible for me.

Times change, and we change with them: so said the ancient Romans. Times change in *circumstances* and people change in *feelings*.

When David the shepherd had no other care but to watch over the flock of his father Jesse in meadows green with grain and speckled with every kind of flower, with the bright sun shining in the cloudless sky and the gleam of the "quiet waters" in the streams and lakes, when he had with him whenever he moved or halted his phial of oil in his pocket and his food for the day, so that his young head was anointed with oil he was provided with a delicious meal in the fields and his cup was overflowing—then he was inspired to utter the 23rd Psalm, calling God his Shepherd and he himself, His sheep who was in need of nothing. When the "valley of the shadow of death" was still far distant from David, he said optimistically and with conviction to his Invisible but Almighty Shepherd, "though I walk through the valley of the shadow of death, I will fear no evil: for thou art with me; thy rod and thy staff they comfort me." But when David became a man and was faced with being the shepherd not of the sheep of Jesse, his earthly father, but of the people of Jehovah, his heavenly Father, who first of all had led him through "the valley of the shadow of death"—not the valley of death, but the valley of its shadow—his bold confidence changed to gloomy pessimism and his joyful hymn of praise was rearranged into a sorrowful song of prayer. Then the "shadow of death," taking on human form, threatened David, and he prayed to His Leader:

"Be merciful unto me, O God: for man would swallow me up; . . . Mine enemies would daily swallow me up." Then this shadow took on the form of lions, and the sheep of the Lord complains to his invisible Shepherd: "My soul is among lions: and I lie even among them that are set on fire, even the sons of men, whose teeth are spears and arrows, and their tongue a sharp sword." Then this shadow of fatal danger altered to an engulfing bog and going through it he wails to his Savior: "Save me, O God; for the waters are come in unto my soul. I sink in deep mire, where there is no standing: I am come into deep waters, where the floods overflow me. (Psalm 56:1-2; Psalm 57:4; Psalm 69:1-2).

Only after he has passed believing and hoping through the "valley of the shadow of death" can he say about God, and with gratitude to God: He "delivered us from so great a death" (from men) (2 Corinthians 1:10); "Notwithstanding the Lord stood with me, and strengthened me . . . I was delivered out of the mouth of the lion (2 Timothy 4:17), and in triumph his spirit can sing the hymn of praise to his Deliverer, Savior and Lord: "I waited patiently for the Lord; and he inclined unto me, and heard my cry. He brought me up also out of an horrible pit, out of the miry clay, and set my feet upon a rock, and established my goings. And he hath put a new song in my mouth, even praise unto our God" (Psalm 40:1-3). Only then does the theoretical human confidence: "I will fear no evil: for thou art with me" (Psalm 23: 4) become the divine, practical fact: "God was with him, And delivered him out of all his afflictions" (Acts 7:9-10).

So it is with all positive and decisive travelers "into the paradise of Canaan, where is the dawn of eternal happiness." So it was with David, Christ's forefather in the flesh, and with all righteous men. So it was with David's descendants in the natural human way, the root of David which God created and with the God-man Jesus Christ (Revelation 22:16) "In the days of his flesh" (Hebrews 5:7), He more than once and in different ways told His disciples about the purpose of His incarnation or taking on human form, which consisted of His expiatory, sacrificial death. He looked on His human flesh as a sacrifice, but His Divinity represented an *eternal* Priest in the strength of the uniqueness of His sacrifice. Posing or appearing as "that great shepherd of the sheep, through the blood of the everlasting covenant (Hebrews 13:20), He announced to His unbelieving hearers "I am the good shepherd . . . and I lay down my life for the sheep . . . No man taketh it from me, but I lay it down of myself. I have power to lay it down, and I have power to take it again" (John 10:14, 15, 18).

Willingness for self-sacrifice and the assertion of all-powerfulness to raise himself from the dead . . . In another instance, declaring to His disciples His eternal priesthood and His sacrifice, universal in its world-wide application, ageless throughout time and all-sufficient in its strength, He said, "The Son of man came not to be ministered unto, but to minister, and to give his life a ransom for many"(Matthew 20:28)—that is, for *all*:

> ◊ I exhort therefore, that, first of all, supplications, prayers, intercessions, and giving of thanks, be made for all men (1 Timothy 2:1)
>
> ◊ But we see Jesus . . . crowned with glory and honour; that he by the grace of God should taste death for every man. (Hebrews 2:9)

◊ For the grace of God that bringeth salvation hath appeared to all men. (Titus 2:11)

Such was the declaration of the God-Man Christ Jesus to both His enemies and His friends when His sacrificed, mortal half was still in complete safety, when the decisive, not merely critical but shattering moment approached, the moment of the entry of the immortal Priest and the mortal sacrifice in One Person no longer into the "valley of the shadow of death," but into the gates of death itself—shameful, terrible, torturing death. He said this when the rope of necessity, thrown on to the neck of the sacrifice, dragged it irresistibly to the place of slaughter. Then the sacrifice, mortally afflicted in soul, His body trembling terribly in a cold sweat, mingled with blood, on a bitterly cold night in early spring, "with strong crying and tears" (Hebrews 5:7) prayed to His Heavenly Father for mercy, saying: "O my Father, if it be possible, let this cup pass from me," but the strong-willed Priest said to the Almighty: "Thy will be done" (Matthew 26:39, 42). The unshakable resolution of the Divine Priest overcame the fear of the trembling human sacrifice—and our redemption was accomplished.

As regards the general redemption of each and every one who wishes for himself salvation from the power of sin and eternal death, one can say in the words of a verse from a Psalm: *Death is annulled, and we are delivered.* In certain cases, however, after bitter Christian experiences endured in the "valley of the shadow of death" *for Christ's sake*, after coming out from it tried in the crucible of misfortunes and afflictions of this life, instead of the one verse just quoted, one can sing with delight the whole 124th Psalm as a hymn of praise to the Leader and Deliverer and as a triumphal song of victory in Christ after gaining a glorious victory over evil *by the strength of him who loved us* (Romans 8:37).

> If it had not been the Lord who was on our side, now may Israel say; If it had not been the Lord who was on our side, when men rose up against us: Then they had swallowed us up quick, when their wrath was kindled against us: Then the waters had overwhelmed us, the stream had gone over our soul: Then the proud waters had gone over our soul. Blessed be the Lord, who hath not given us as a prey to their teeth. Our soul is escaped as a bird out of the snare of the fowlers: the snare is broken, and we are escaped. Our help is in the name of the Lord, who made heaven and earth. (Psalm 124:1-8)

You, dear Peter Yakovlevich, like other brothers confessing the faith who have passed through "the valley of the shadow of death" under the leadership and protection of Him who "was dead; and, behold . . . alive for evermore, (Revelation 1:18), and to whom from the moment of His glorious resurrection from the dead now and for evermore "all power is given . . . in heaven and in earth" (Matthew 28:18), from personal experience can bear testimony better than all of us who have not passed through to the truth of the words of Psalm 22:4 and Matthew 28:18.

I understand from your letter that I. I. Bondarenko and V. I. Kolesnikov have been overtaken by the same illness as our Sasha. Did I understand you correctly? Sasha's situation is the same as before. The crisis of the illness cannot yet be seen.

I close with greetings to you, to our esteemed Lydia Mikhailovna and little Georgi, to S. V. Petrov and all the dear ones in the blood of Christ and the Spirit of the Living God. Pray for us.

With sincere affection and respect,

G. Shipkov.

Third Letter (Fragment)

People are bitterly disillusioned about swift help from God and usually first fall into despair and then into godlessness. In this way, their faith, like a spark from a crucible, first of all soars gleaming upward to the heavens, then is extinguished in the night air and falls as a speck of dust to the cold earth. Alas for such "believers"!

This is not the kind of faith in God and the kind of hope in His all-powerfulness and mercy that true Christians and reborn children of God should have. The central pillar in the church of God's grace looks on the trial of believers by afflictions as a purifying fire, melting gold to give it greater value (1 Peter 1:3-7). Gold in the smelting furnace is not destroyed but is purified and gains in value. True faith is subject to the same process and attains the same result in the crucible of trial by afflictions. Another pillar of the same church orders believers to have not a simple but a great joy when they fall into many various trials, for the testing of their faith, leading to an increase of steadfastness, which has its full effect on those who are tried (James 1:2-4). And finally, the third pillar of the Gentile section of the same church reasons that the gift of God we have received, Faith, with its accompanying afflictions, evolves, not decreasing, but increasing in new experiences and raising itself by degrees higher and higher to the faultless sensation of the love of God, poured out in the hearts of believers by the Holy Spirit given to them in the day they turn to the Lord (Romans 5:1-5). On the basis of such an experience, the apostle asks: "Who shall separate us from the love of Christ? Shall tribulation, or distress, or persecution, or famine, or nakedness, or peril, or sword?" (Romans 8:35). And at once, he answers with complete conviction:

> I am persuaded, that neither death, nor life, nor angels [fallen], nor principalities [those in command], nor powers [authorities], nor things present, nor things

> to come, nor height [worldly position], nor depth [humiliation in the world], nor any other creature, shall be able to separate us from the love of God, which is in Christ Jesus our Lord. (Romans 8:38-39)

From the very beginning of Christianity, to us believers "it is given in the behalf of Christ, not only to believe on him, but also to suffer for his sake" (Philippians 1:29). His redemptive sufferings for believers must necessarily be compensated for by their sufferings in thanks to Him.

ALEXANDER SHALASHOV

Remember them which have the rule over you, who have spoken unto you the word of God: whose faith follow, considering the end of their conversation. (Hebrews13:7)

Nineteen seventy-one saw the eightieth anniversary of the birth of Alexander Afanasevich Shalashov, an evangelist of the Volgo-Kamsky Evangelical Christian-Baptist Union from 1920 to 1928, a member of the Organizing Committee of Evangelical Christians-Baptists during 1962-1963, and pastor of the Chelyabinsk church. He passed into eternity on December 7th, 1963.

Alexander Afanasevich did much blessed work in God's harvest field and endured imprisonment and great trials for the name of Christ. For eighteen years, he was ill and bedridden, then he was healed by the Lord and sent to the work of the spiritual revival of the Evangelical-Baptist brotherhood.

Many believers remember Alexander Afanasevich with love—a kind, simple, sympathetic Christian, a faithful, courageous, tried and tested servant of God, a man of principle in questions of faith, who stood up dauntlessly in defense of the work of evangelism at a critical moment when there was a breach in the house of God.

Alexander Afanasevich was born on June 4th, 1891 in the town of Minora in Chelyabinsk region. In 1915, he came to believe in the Lord and subsequently underwent baptism in Khabarovsk Evangelical Christian-Baptist Church. Having joined Christ's church, Alexander Afanasevich dedicated his whole life to preaching the Gospel.

In 1919, be was ordained by brother D. S. Olshansky in Samara (now Kuibyshev) to serve as an evangelist. During the ten years from 1919 to 1929, Alexander Afanasevich worked zealously in the Volgo-Kamsky Evangelical Christian-Baptist Union, preaching and organizing the churches of God in Povolzhe and the Urals.

At the same time, Alexander Afanasevich took a lively interest in the spiritual life of his own Far East brotherhood, where he had become a believer.

The journal *Evangelist*, which was printed in Vladivostok, in 1921 published a letter from Alexander Afanasevich under the heading:

> Kiev farm
> Ufimsky district
>
> We wish that the Lord may open up to you His good heavenly treasure house and give abundant gifts to all His children in the Far East.
>
> Next, a warm greeting to all those who love the Lord and who know me personally. I became a believer and promised to serve my Lord in Khabarovsk in 1915.
>
> Dear brother R. A.! Our esteemed and long-awaited journal, preaching peace, which you sent, has once more reached us

living here in pagan Galilee, at the foot of the Urals. Tears of divine happiness shone in our eyes when we saw it, and we listened once more to its words with an attentive ear.

After a long and tiring wait, we have heard the words of many witnesses of the Gospel truth and have again refreshed the thirsting soul (Proverbs 25:25). Once more the clearly printed words of the work of God's children have shone before us, and we have gathered in the house around the good *Evangelist*. We have listened avidly to the news from a distant land, but our native land, of how the children of God are bearing the heat, affliction, and horrors of the day and rejoice as at the gathering in of the vine.

O, God grant that this joy may not cease forever, although "the fig tree shall not blossom, neither shall fruit be in the vines; the labour of the olive shall fail, and the fields shall yield no meat; the flock shall be cut off from the fold, and there shall be no herd in the stalls: Yet I will rejoice in the Lord, I will joy in the God of my salvation" (Habakkuk 3:17-19)

I remain your warmly affectionate friend, the least of the co-laborers in God's work.

A. Shalashov.

(From the journal *Evangelist*, No. 5, May 1921, p. 79.)

In 1929, the persecutions began. The Volgo-Kamsky Union was closed. During these years, Alexander Afanasevich continued to preach the Gospel in communities in the towns of Artemovsk, Mosdok, and Makhachkaly. At the same time, he worked as a blacksmith. In 1934, as a result of occupational injury, Alexander Afanasevich was paralyzed for many long years.

However, despite his serious illness which kept him entirely bedridden, he was arrested in 1936 as a servant of God and lay for five years in the prison hospital in Kharkov.

After his release from prison in 1941, Alexander Afanasevich remained bedridden until 1956. These were hard years both for himself and for his wife, Lukeria Filippovna. But even under these conditions Alexander Afanasevich wanted to be useful for the work of the Lord. His house in Mozdok, and later in Uman and Chelyabinsk, became a place for believers to visit. Many came to him for advice and encouragement. Many prayed for the healing of this dear servant. The Lord heard His children's prayers, and so in 1956 after eighteen years of serious ailment, Alexander Afanasevich rose from his sickbed. The Lord healed him and once again entrusted him with a great service to the Church.

The believers of Chelyabinsk elected him their pastor, and he performed this ministry until the day of his death.

The Chelyabinsk church endured great trials. In 1958, their prayer house was taken away, and the 300 believers of Chelyabinsk were forced to gather for worship in various private houses, but even these meetings were constantly subject to persecution.

When the Action Group of Evangelical Christians-Baptists was formed in1961, the Chelyabinsk church was one of the first to respond to God's summons to revival. Alexander Afanasevich, a faithful servant of God, grown wise with great spiritual experience, supported the work of the Action Group with his whole soul.

Even before the beginning of the work of the Action Group and the Organizing Committee, Alexander Afanasevich had carried on a great spiritual work among the unregistered churches of the Urals in regulating their services, in the election and ordination of pastors, and in the uniting of the Evangelical Christian-Baptist churches of the Urals among themselves. The believers of the Urals felt great love for Alexander Afanasevich.

In 1962, he was elected to the Organizing Committee of Evangelical Christians-Baptists as the representative of the churches of the Urals. Despite his old age, Alexander Afanasevich took a most active part in the work of the Organizing Committee. He visited a large number of the churches of the Urals, the central regions of Russia, the Ukraine, and Siberia. He ordained many young ministers during 1962 and 1963 for the great work of spiritual revival in our brotherhood

An old experienced worker of the Volgo-Kamsky Evangelical Christian-Baptist Union, making use of his deserved authority among the brotherhood, Alexander Afanasevich together with Sergei Terentevich Golev and Matvei Petrovich Kondrashov was as it were the connecting link between the old generation of faithful servants of the Evangelical-Baptist brotherhood, who for the most part had laid down their lives in the camps, and the new generation, called by the Lord to service in the 'sixties.

Alexander Afanasevich possessed great charm of soul; people's hearts clung to him, and it was a joy to talk to him. He had an especially moving fatherly love to Gennadi Konstantinovich Kryuchkov, who performed his ministry in very complex and straitened circumstances, undergoing constant persecution. Every time they met again after trips around the churches Alexander Afanasevich would embrace brother Kryuchkov with tears in his eyes and say joyfully, "You're alive! And safe! And free! Praise God!"

Alexander Afanasevich had a fine powerful bass voice. I remember that one day after one of our fraternal conferences in 1963, he sang his favorite hymn: "O, no, no one in the universe will deprive the faithful of their freedom!" It was good to watch this old man, gray with age, courageous, tempered in trials for the faith of Christ, now raised up once again in the breach in the house of God!

In 1962-1963, Alexander Afanasevich put his signature to several very important documents of the Organizing Committee of Evangelical Christians-Baptists. In these years, thousands of believers of registered and unregistered Evangelical Christian-Baptist churches were petitioning the government in writing for permission to convene an Evangelical Christian-Baptist congress under the leadership of the Organizing Committee.

In October 1963, the Council for the Affairs of Religious Cults, wishing to put an end to the campaign of petitions for a congress, and disregarding the will of the petitioners, permitted the All-Union Council to hold an all-union conference, subsequently renamed a congress.

The aim of the All-Union Council, however, was to lead the whole Evangelical Christian-Baptist brotherhood into error by the means of holding a fictitious congress (a pseudo-congress) and to condemn the Organizing Committee's campaign for a congress. Four hundred men with the right to vote attended the conference. Delegates' passes for the congress were distributed to them, a congress agenda was produced, there were reports, accounts, speeches, elections and so on—all this was meant to create the illusion of a genuine congress. The participants in the conference were accommodated in the Moscow hotel "Turist," buses were allotted for their disposal, and so on. But at that time, the true initiators of the congress were languishing in the prisons and camps of the land.

The Council for Religious Affairs and the All-Union Council had prepared well for their congress. This is how one of the prisoners wrote about it:

> Some men slept peacefully in a hotel,
> Other men dozed on plank beds:
> Some abandoned Christ's commands,
> Others suffered for the faith.

The Organizing Committee sent its representatives to this conference, headed by Alexander Afanasevich.

Cold autumn rain was failing. The believers, about fifty of them, stood in front of the All-Union Council building in Moscow. Among them was a tall old man in a raincoat, leaning on a stick—Alexander Afanasevich. He was not allowed into the building and stood in the rain outside for more than an hour.

After this, he became seriously ill. At the end of October 1963, a group of brothers and sisters saw Alexander Afanasevich off to his home. He left from Paveletsky station in Moscow. Everyone sensed that this was their last meeting, their parting with the dear old minister. The brothers and sisters wanted to see once more his good, brave face, to hear for the last time his fatherly parting words.

Suddenly into the station waiting room came Gennadi Kryuchkov. He had also come to say farewell to his dear comrade in the ministry. Alexander Afanasevich became agitated and said, "Why have you come here? Why, they're looking for you everywhere. They could arrest you right here! Go away!"

When we had seated him in the carriage and we ourselves were crowding round the window, Alexander Afanasevich waved his hand to us for the last time and on the glass of the window traced out several times, 1 Peter 5:1-3. We could not receive his pastor's blessing and good wishes without tears. The train moved off taking dear Alexander Afanasevich away from us. One of the sisters from the Ukraine accompanied him as far as Chelyabinsk.

We went away sadly from the station . . .

When he arrived home in Chelyabinsk Alexander Afanasevich took to his bed for the last time. He asked that on the wall opposite his bed should be hung the small bag which held his Bible, and that his stick should be stood there. These were his invariable companions in his journeys throughout the country. He often looked at them, remembering his numerous visits to believers.

Alexander Afanasevich's friends and relatives felt that his heart was straining toward the church, to God's boundless harvest field where there was so much work to be done.

However, our old brother realized that his earthly path was coming to an end, that the Lord was recalling him, now that he had turned gray in the struggle for the truth, into His everlasting dwelling place. In these days, many friends in the faith and in ministry visited Alexander Afanasevich. He encouraged everyone and strengthened them spiritually, urging them to act courageously for the faith of the Gospel.

In the first days of December 1963, Alexander Afanasevich received two notices from the KGB in Chelyabinsk—summonses for questioning. But he was so weak that he could not visit this institution which displayed so great an interest in believers.

On December 7th, 1963, Alexander Afanasevich passed into eternity.

He left us all a good example of Christian longsuffering, gentleness, faithfulness to the Lord, selflessness, and courage in the face of persecutions and trials. For very many believers, he was a good father and preceptor. His pastor's parting words from the first Epistle of Peter have always remained in the memory of the servants of the revived church:

> The elders which are among you I exhort . . . Feed the flock of God which is among you, taking the oversight thereof, not by constraint, but willingly; not for filthy lucre, but of a ready mind; Neither as being lords over God's heritage, but being examples to the flock. (1 Peter 5:1-3)

PAVEL ZAKHAROV

May the grace and peace of God in the Holy Spirit increase greatly in you, my dear and beloved friends. I greet you with feelings of deep love and a sincere heart, I the least of you, who was among you but now am separated, like many friends in Christ.

May His strength in you increase and may you be able to bear all abuse for His work. The Lord be with you always and in everything.

Dear friends, remember me and all of us prisoners in your prayers. We believe that the Lord is our justification, and He will overcome those who struggle with him and will stand up in defense of His suffering people. Give greetings to all the brothers and sisters who labor and to all who love the Lord. May His will be done to the glory of His name.

Yours sincerely, the least of all.

Pavel Zakharov

This is an extract from a letter by Pavel Frolovich Zakharov, a Christian prisoner, which was passed in 1964 to brothers serving on the Organizing Committee of Evangelical Christians-Baptists from the Potma labor camp in Mordovia.

It was a good and long-awaited piece of news from our dear brother and co-laborer in God's harvest field, whose life and service were inseparably linked with the work of spiritual revival in the Evangelical-Baptist brotherhood. We were encouraged by our prisoner brother's cheerful spirit and by his hope in God's might. Over the last ten years, Pavel Zakharov has twice been in prison. After each release, he joined in the labor in God's harvest field.

But now our brother is not with us. On July 1st, 1971, Pavel Zakharov's heart was stilled, and he passed away. The hearts of his friends and relatives were wrung with grief: but he left an example of faithfulness to the Lord.

Our dear brother endured much suffering for the faith of Christ. On February 24th, 1945 (age 22), he was arrested, as a Christian, for the first time, and was sentenced by a *troika* to five years' imprisonment. He served this term in "Ivdal" camp in the Urals.

In 1950, after the end of his five-year term, Zakharov was sent into exile to the north of Krasnoyarsk district. In 1954, he returned from exile and settled in the town of Zhdanov in the Ukraine. Here also, however, he was subjected to a search of his house (in May 1955) and to threats.

In 1955, Zakharov moved to the town of Prokopievsk in Siberia. Here he took part zealously in the ministry of the local church as a preacher, a precentor, and later an ordained evangelist.

In 1961, when the call to revival in our brotherhood was heard, Pavel Zakharov, along with the whole Evangelical Christian-Baptist church in Prokopievsk, responded to God's summons.

However, the enemies of God's work were not asleep. On October 20th, 1962, the Rudichni Executive Committee of Prokopievsk passed a resolution demanding the exile of P. F. Zakharov for five years because of his preaching activity.

But the Lord preserved him from exile.

In 1962, he was elected by the believers of Siberia to serve on the Organizing Committee of Evangelical Christians-Baptists. The period from 1962 to February 1964 was especially fruitful in Pavel Zakharov's ministry. During these years, he visited hundreds of registered and unregistered communities in Siberia, Kazakhstan, Central Asia, the Urals, European Russia, the Ukraine, and the Baltic region.

Pavel Zakharov participated with fervor in the publication of the journal *Herald of Salvation*. The very name of the journal was borrowed from a poem he had written.

In February 1964, Pavel Zakharov was arrested in Irkutsk. During the search, photographs of Nikolai Khmara (1916-1964), who had been tortured to death in prison, and a letter from the Barnaul church reporting a crime that had been committed, were taken away from him.

The Irkutsk procuracy charged Zakharov with slander on account of the above-mentioned documents and brought him to trial under article 70 of the Criminal Code of the RSFSR. Zakharov was sentenced to three years of labor camp, strict regime. He was sent to the Potma labor camp in Mordovia. At that time brother N. P. Khrapov was serving a sentence in this camp, and there were also several other Evangelical Christian-Baptist believers there. It was from here that Pavel Zakharov sent us his letter. It was hidden in a shoe and carried out of the camp.

In December 1964, Pavel Zakharov was released and rehabilitated by a resolution of the Supreme Soviet of the USSR dated November 10th, 1964, "In the absence of *corpus delicti*."

Thus, the veracity of the letter from the Barnaul church and the authenticity of the photographs of brother Khmara who was tortured for his faith were officially and legally corroborated.

At this period, the church was urgently praying and energetically petitioning outsiders for the release of Christian prisoners. Delegations of believers from many local Evangelical Christian-Baptist communities arrived in Moscow: from Kiev, Brest, Bryansk,

«Брат Хмара за несколько лет до смерти».

Вопиющим явился случай верующего ЕХБ Хмары. Отец 4-х малолетних детей был в заключении умерщвлен. Об этом стало известно, после того как его семья, получив сообщение о его кончине и выпросив его тело для погребения, обнаружила на его ногах следы ожогов каленым железом, а во рту тряпичный кляп, за которым не оказалось языка. Приводятся фотографические снимки.

A photo of Nikolai Khmara and one of his family: Posthumous photos of Nicholas Hmara were seized during searches from believers.

Chelyabinsk, Barnaul, and other towns. As a rule, the delegations were not large, about five to ten men.

In 1964, the Council of Prisoners' Relatives of the Evangelical Christian-Baptist Church was formed in defense of those convicted for the Word of God. The Council sent direct petitions to the Procuracy of the USSR. In 1964, throughout almost six months representatives of the Organizing Committee of Evangelical Christian-Baptists were to be found in the waiting room of the Central Committee of the Communist Party of the Soviet Union with petitions against the intervention of the Council for the Affairs of Religious Cults and other bodies in the internal church life of the whole Evangelical-Baptist brotherhood.

In the second half of 1964 began the rehabilitation and release of Evangelical Christian-Baptist prisoners. At the beginning of 1965, almost all of them had been released, with the exception of a few people. The Lord had answered His people's prayers. The church of God rejoiced and praised its Heavenly Father.

> When the Lord turned again the captivity of Zion, we were like them that dream. Then was our mouth filled with laughter, and our tongue with singing: then said they among the heathen, The Lord hath done great things for them. The Lord hath done great things for us; whereof we are glad. (Psalm 126:1-3)

Those coming out of prison joined zealously in the labor in God's harvest field. Returning from prison in December 1964, Pavel Zakharov visited many churches of our brotherhood, calling the believers to act unanimously for the faith of the Gospel.

During this period, he did much work throughout Siberia and accomplished visits to many churches in the Northern Caucasus. He gave a great deal of his energy and attention to the local church in Prokopievsk.

In 1966, however, a new period of persecution began. In 1966, new decrees were published directed against believers. In the provinces, open persecution began with new arrests of believers.

In May 1966, a large delegation of Evangelical Christian-Baptist believers arrived in Moscow. Among them was Pavel Zakharov, as a delegate from the believers of Prokopievsk. At ten o'clock in the morning in front of the main entrance to the building of the Central Committee of the CPSU, there suddenly appeared a large delegation of believers numbering about five hundred people. The delegation spent two days and one night outside of the Central Committee Building, petitioning for all those persecuted and oppressed for their faith. On May 17th, 1966, the peaceful delegation of believers was arrested and taken to Lefortovo prison in Moscow. Among those arrested was Pavel Zakharov.

On June 23rd, 1966, the Pervomaisky People's Court sentenced Zakharov under article 142 section 2 of the Criminal Code of the RSFSR to three years in labor camp, intensive regime.

Zakharov spent the last three years of his imprisonment in the town of Nalchik in the Northern Caucasus. His health took an abrupt turn for the worse. When he returned from prison, he spent many months in a hospital.

In October 1969, a great tragedy overtook him: his wife, Esfir Yakovlevna, died. Their four children were left motherless.

Although he was ill, Pavel Zakharov continued to perform what service he could for the church in Prokopievsk.

In July I970, in the hospital in Prokopievsk, Zakharov wrote the article, "The Last Supper." I quote a few excerpts from his article:

> We wait for His appearance and the rapture of the church—His Bride. Wait thus for Christ at all times, as long as there is breath in you and you can hear the beating of your heart in your decrepit body.

> O dear friend, brother and sister!—Awake!
>
> And now while you still hear the voice of the Merciful One, who is patiently awaiting your return, return quickly! Fall down before Him! Bring the talent the Lord has given you with the profit that pleases Him. He expects sacrificial service from you, from me, and from everyone who comes to His house. The church prays to the Lord for her servants, who so much need His strength and leadership. She prays that the Lord will still raise up worthy servants for His vineyard.
>
> The church prays to the Lord that the Gospel may spread and be preached everywhere and rejoices because for her witness to Christ, she suffers contempt, imprisonment, exile, and every kind of deprivation from the world. She thanks her heavenly Father for the strength of the Spirit of God, which gives victory over every dishonor and evil.

This was his spiritual testament to the Prokopievsk church and the whole Evangelical Christian-Baptist brotherhood.

In 1971, Pavel Zakharov's state of health worsened abruptly and on July 1st, he passed away at 49 years old.

Pavel Zakharov walked along a difficult but faithful path. Selflessly, he sowed the seeds of God's eternal truth among the Russian people. Thousands of people heard his sermons and his calls to faithfulness to the Lord.

In prison cells and labor camps among the prisoners, he bore a fearless testimony to God's love. They respected Pavel Zakharov and affectionately named him "Dad"!

> They that sow in tears shall reap in joy. He that goeth forth and weepeth, bearing precious seed, shall doubtless

> come again with rejoicing, bringing his sheaves with him.
> (Psalm 126:5-6)

These verses also relate to Pavel Zakharov. He is now in Heaven with the Lord. The tears and sorrows of the earthly path have remained far behind. The sheaves of his labor are before the Lord. There, he waits for us too, his friends and comrades in evangelistic labor.

He has already found rest from his labors, but for us, storms and tempests and toil lie in wait on the path to eternity!

Part III: Faithful Christian Women in Russia

Who can find a virtuous woman? for her price is far above rubies. The heart of her husband doth safely trust in her, so that he shall have no need of spoil. She will do him good and not evil all the days of her life. (Proverbs 31:10-12)

ALEXANDRA SEMIRECH

I have happy memories of our dear sister in the Lord, Alexandra Ivanovna Semirech.

A simple Russian woman with a strong face, stocky, with robust health and a gruff, almost masculine voice, she had a kind, sensitive heart and a deep and sincere faith in God. She also possessed exceptional courage and the ability to encourage timid and weakened Christians in the years of persecution.

Alexandra Ivanovna was descended from native Siberians, hardened in the struggle with the grim forces of nature and the adversities of life. She lived almost all her life in Omsk. She became a believer when she was married and had three children. Her husband was a confirmed drunkard who did her much harm. But she did a great deal of good for her husband and her family, and for many believers.

Alexandra Ivanovna's house was a refuge for many persecuted and outcast people. With goodwill and zeal, she continued in our days the ministry of Gaius, the host to strangers (Romans 16:23).

From 1937-1938, the blind poetess Polina Yakovlevna Skakunova lived in her house. She had broken with atheism in the 'twenties and had wandered around a good deal, and in 1938, she was arrested for confessing faith in Christ.

From 1941-1944, the two children of the Christian prisoner Ivanov-Klyshnikov were in her house after the arrest of his wife, Anna Petrovna.

From I943, Alexandra Ivanovna together with another sincere and virtuous Christian woman, Yevdokiya Samoilovna Varnavskaya, sought out believing prisoners in one of the camps situated on the outskirts of the town. They were members of a group of Christian young people arrested in the Crimea in 1940 for conducting a Christian young people's meeting and sentenced to five to ten years. In the difficult years of the war, Alexandra Ivanovna and Yevdokiya Samoilovna apportioned food for parcels for these Christian prisoners from their own modest shares.

From 1943-1944, Alexandra Ivanovna was one of the most active and fervent organizers of the renewal of regular meetings for worship in Omsk. A simple, uneducated woman, she was a fiery preacher of the Gospel at the Omsk meetings.

At the end of 1961, by which time she was extremely old, she traveled to Chelyabinsk to establish links with the Action Group of the Evangelical Christian-Baptist Church. Alexander Afanasevich Shalashov told me about this: he was the pastor of Chelyabinsk church and is now at rest with the Lord.

Shortly after this she went away peacefully to the Lord.

Peace be with you, dear laborer for the Lord!

POLINA SKAKUNOVA

In the years before the war, the blind Christian poetess Polina Yakovlevna Skakunova was well known to the believers of Povolzhe and Siberia.

In the 'twenties, Polina Yakovlevna and her husband were literary workers and lived in Saratov. Polina Yakovlevna was an active atheist. She traveled through the villages of Saratov region giving atheist lectures.

"We don't need God" she used to say. "Man himself is the forger of his own happiness. I shall live as I want to live!"

In 1925, Polina Yakovlevna's husband suddenly died. This was a terrible blow for her. After the funeral, when everyone had dispersed from the cemetery, she returned to her husband's grave and attempted to commit suicide. The cemetery watchman heard a shot at night. Some inner voice forced him to get up, dress, and go to the place where the shot had sounded. Among the wreaths on the fresh grave, he found Polina Yakovlevna covered in blood and unconscious. He called some people to help and took her to hospital. Polina Yakovlevna had shot at her temple but had not achieved what she desired. She survived, but damaged both her eyes with the shot and went blind.

Polina Yakovlevna gave way to despair and became embittered. In a conversation with a believer in Saratov in 1925, she said: "It has turned out that I could not live as I warned . . . to make up for it I shall die as I want!" She was stubborn and did not mean to live: she opened her veins, took poison, and even attempted to throw herself under a train.

But the Lord in His great love prevented her.

After some while, terribly ill and disfigured, Polina Yakovlevna became more calm and began to look for a new kind of occupation for herself. Unbelieving friends advised her to occupy herself with atheist literary work, for which she was taken several times to a prayer house of Evangelical Christians-Baptists in Saratov. Making her way toward the meeting for the first time, she said, "I'll go, if only to laugh at them!" But the result was quite the opposite. The blind woman saw the spiritual beauty of Christ and believed in Him with all the strength of her sensitive soul worn out by suffering. She repented of her former sinful life and her attempts at suicide, was baptized, and began to witness to Christ.

Polina Yakolevna wrote a wonderful poem about her turning to the Lord and a great number of outstanding Christian verses. Before the war, they went the rounds of believers in numerous copies.

Her unbelieving friends forsook her; she was deprived of her means of subsistence, but she did not renounce Christ.

For a while, she lived in Omsk with Alexandra Semirech, who surrounded her with truly motherly love and care.

I remember Polina Yakovlevna—a thin intelligent woman with black spectacles covering empty eye-sockets. In 1938, I was ill for half the winter with pneumonia. On many days, Polina Yakovlevna sat at my bedside. I remember her kind hand straightening the blanket and giving me medicine, I remember her quiet voice when she read her poems about Christ to me, a ten-year-old boy, and had heart-to-heart talks with me about Him.

In 1939, Polina Yakovlevna was arrested in Omsk and did not return. She died an unknown death in prison. What danger did she represent for atheism?

A very great danger, obviously: she kindled people's hearts by her inner spiritual insight, her deep faith, and her poems about Christ.

ALEXANDRA MOZGOVA

On March 9th, 1972 in Moscow, Alexandra Ivanovna Mozgova passed into eternity at the age of sixty-seven. The Lord called this tireless and faithful laborer to His everlasting dwelling place.

She turned to the Lord when she was sixteen and began to labor in His vineyard. During the time of the revolution, she recited invocatory poems on the squares of Moscow in front of large crowds of listeners. In these years, the preaching of Christ overflowed like a broad river across the plains of Russia. Thousands of sinners turned to Christ

In 1926, Alexandra Ivanovna Mozgova began to work in the office of the Federal Union of Christians-Baptists in Moscow. All the work of the Baptist Union in those years was subordinated to two chief tasks: the evangelization of the country and the inner spiritual education of the swiftly growing Evangelical Christian-Baptist brotherhood.

Alexandra Ivanovna was greatly influenced spiritually by the blessed laborers in the harvest field of the Gospel—Nikolai Odintsov, Pavel Datsko, Pavel Ivanov-Klyshnikov, and others. Throughout her life, she retained not only radiant memories of them, but also faithfulness to the Holy Gospel for which they had given their lives. She often remembered their fervent prayers, their zealous, selfless service, and their deep personal attachment to one another.

After 1929, when the blows of persecution fell upon our brotherhood, and the leaders of the Baptist Union were subjected to particularly intense pressure on the part of the authorities, Nikolai Odintsov would often gather his colleagues in the office around him after a regular summons to the secret police, share with them the difficulties which had arisen, and pray fervently with them for the dear brotherhood. He taught his brothers and sisters who worked with him steadfastness and courage in upholding the things of God. When the blows of persecution affected each of Odintsov's colleagues personally, his young sister-colleagues almost all went to prison but kept their faithfulness to Christ.

My parents knew Alexandra Ivanovna well. In 1930, during the work of the Plenum of the Baptist Union in Moscow, my father and mother stayed in her flat at 9 Rubtsovy Lane. The same year my father was arrested in that flat . . .

A few decades later, I also had the opportunity to make Alexandra Ivanovna's acquaintance. With great emotion, I crossed the threshold of the old Moscow flat where my father's prison journey had begun in 1930.

Nikolai Odintsov was arrested in November 1933, and Alexandra Ivanovna was arrested almost simultaneously. During the investigation, she maintained total silence about the life of our brotherhood. She was sentenced together with Odintsov to three years. She served her term in a camp for the construction of the White Sea-Baltic canal in Medvezhegorsk district. A. Ananin, the Chairman of the Siberian Christian-Baptist Union, also served his sentence there. Alexandra Ivanovna was able to see him. According to certain information, he was still alive in 1946, but after that his fate is unknown . . . He did not return from the camp. His wife

Varvara Ivanovna was arrested in Siberia in December 1941 and also did not return.

In 1936, Alexandra Ivanovna completed her term. But she remained in Karelia until summer 1941. In autumn 1941, she was evacuated to Moscow.

In October 1944, a unifying conference of leading workers of Evangelical Christians-Baptists was held in Moscow. It was not a large conference; only about forty people attended. The majority of the participants in the conference had been quickly released from prisons and camps not long before.

One thing caused great bewilderment: why were such ministers as A. Ananin and many others not at the conference, who in those years were still alive and languishing in the camps?

It has been suggested that the authorities imposed certain conditions on the servants of the church in the camps, which Christian conscience did not allow many brothers to accept . . . and thus, they remained there to die.

Alexandra Ivanovna, who at that time was living in the capital, was also present at the conference in Moscow. Since 1944, she had begun to work in the office of the newly formed All-Union Council of Evangelical Christians-Baptists. Of course, the atmosphere among the workers of the All-Union Council was quite different to that of Odintsov's time. The leaders of the All-Union Council resolved questions about their ministry not on their knees before the Lord, but in the offices of the Council for the Affairs of Religious Cults and of other bodies. This finally led them in 1960 to publish the well-known anti-Evangelical documents, the *Statutes and the Letters of Instruction to Senior Presbyters.* In 1960, the All-Union Council carried out a purge of its staff; Alexandra Ivanovna was pensioned off.

In 1961, the work of the Action Group of the Evangelical Christians-Baptists was begun. Alexandra Ivanovna followed it attentively and with deep sympathy, praying fervently to the Lord for the revival of the Evangelical-Baptist brotherhood, and then she herself began to help the friends of the revival. During 1965 and 1966, she greatly helped the Council of Evangelical Christian-Baptist Churches with typewriting work, especially at the time when the Regulations of the Council of Churches were being worked out. Alexandra Ivanovna played an active part in the *Herald of Salvation*, the journal of the revived brotherhood of Evangelical Christians-Baptists. She gleaned a great deal of material for the journal. She carefully preserved a whole series of unique manuscripts of articles and poetry written by Evangelical laborers of past years, and subsequently handed them over to the Council of Churches.

A member of the registered Evangelical Christian-Baptist community in Moscow, Alexandra Ivanovna upheld Evangelical-Baptist principles. Often, she exposed the leadership of the All-Union Council and the leaders of the local Moscow community in deviations from the Gospel. But her quiet, faint voice was often, raised alone.

In 1966, when numerous trials of supporters of the Council of Churches were taking place in Moscow, Alexandra Ivanovna was present at almost every trial, sympathizing with and praying for every prisoner.

She knew the history of our brotherhood well, loved the Lord ardently, and saw in the Council of Churches movement the continuation of that great work of the Gospel to which Prokhanov, Odintsov, Ivanov-Klyshnikov, Datsko, and many others had entirely dedicated themselves.

Alexandra Ivanovna lived a long, fruitful life, totally dedicated to the Lord.

In conclusion, I shall quote excerpts from Alexandra Ivanovna's album. For many decades, she kept an album with entries and good wishes from many believers. It opens on March 11th, 1929 with an entry from a student on a Bible course—brother Borets.

The spring of 1929 was the threshold of persecution. The Lord was preparing His church for its trials. These precious brotherly entries and good wishes, preserved since the 'thirties, reveal to us now the exalted spirit of the champions of the Gospel, their courage, and the depth of their faith. Their courageous summons to faithfulness is especially dear to us, the believers of the 'seventies.

From Alezandra Mozgova's Album

Follow thou me. (John 21:22)

The Lord is now opening before His children the fiery door of trial. We can already hear the echoes of the many-visage beast: "To the stake with them!" The children of God must learn in reality what it means to be "hated of all men for my name's sake." But let not our hearts be troubled, for as He opens this door to us, He Himself goes with us, and therefore, as the first Christians did, we too can say, "You can kill us, but you cannot harm us!"

And so let us rejoice, my dear friend Alexandra Ivanovna, that the Lord accords us the honor of participation in the afflictions of His body so that we may subsequently be participants in His glory.

N. Borets
Moscow, Baptist Bible Course
March 11th, 1929

A true witness delivereth souls. (Proverbs 14:25)

V. I. Sinitsin
Moscow
March 9th, 1929

Dear sister Shura!
With our present experiences and feelings, I somehow cannot find it in my heart to write anything joyful. But when I write in someone's album, I want only to express sincere and heartfelt good wishes for their journey along our hard Christian path.

My dear sister, you have already begun to walk along this difficult, sorrow-filled path. Understand then that if you are faithful to the end to your Lord, then also to the end you will not meet with compassion from this world, nor will you find that it understands you. Do not forget this one thing, that while God loves us, the world hates us; and while Heaven accepts us, we will without fail be exiles here. There is no place for us here, there is no cool shade, no shelter to rest from our labors, but we shall be received by Heaven and have a place there.

But this is the world, and when you start to draw near to Golgotha, then even your friends can desert you. One can often encounter this on the Christian path. When all this overtakes you on the path, do not cease to be faithful to the Lord and to serve Him. Bear offenses patiently as though they were not heavy. Forgive everyone. If your friends desert you and your heart is heavy, then weep quietly alone with the Lord, and it will be lighter. Be affectionate and gentle to everyone, and may your meekness and humility, which all of us should possess, be known to everyone. Love everyone with brotherly love, and each person will see Christ in your soul and in your eyes. Always be bold before everyone in this ministry, because in this is our mission. Labor with success and be happy.

V. G. Lobkov
(from Siberia)
March 10th, 1929

Dear sister in the Lord, Mozgova.
To him that overcometh will I give to eat of the tree of life, which is in the midst of the paradise of God. (Revelation 2:7)

F. Sapozhnikov
Moscow
March 9th, 1929

Three wonderful promises:
"The LORD . . . he it is that doth go before thee;
He will be with thee,
He will not fail thee." Deuteronomy 31:8

The first is a sure pledge of security. The second is an inexhaustible fount of encouragement and consolation. The third is a reliable guarantee of unfailing love. He will go before you everywhere, will be with you always, will never fail you.

N. Odintsov
December 13th, 1932

A Good Memory of Our Meeting in Exile
People enter in an album such words as will serve as an expression of the best wishes in life for a person who is close to them in the aspirations whose principles draw them together. These wishes reflect the sentiments and experiences of the present writer.

When I hear wonderful stories about the life and work of individuals who have set themselves as their highest aim the fulfillment of the will of Him who sent us into this life, I am enraptured by their ardent and inspired transports of spirit, pressing them on to super-human feats of self-sacrifice in the name of the Lord Jesus Christ, the Savior of the world, and for the sake of the good and the salvation of their neighbors.

Firm faith in God and devotion to Him to the end (Revelation 2:10), unshakable courage in actions and in various experiences, courage which accompanied all the heroic martyrs of radiant Christianity down the centuries as they marched joyfully to Golgotha, perfect Christian love, the foundation and abundant source of virtue in its different manifestations; bright hope in the precious promises of our Heavenly Father (John 14:23) which instills quiet rest, joy, and peace into the heart; this was the substance of the lives of all those who followed the Leader and Savior of the world—the Lord Jesus Christ.

And to you, dear sister in the Lord, Alexandra Ivanovna, with a sincere heart, I wish that you may acquire from the Almighty Lord God those lofty Christian values which serve as an adornment of the life of a believing person who is marching to the eternal Canaan. In conclusion, Philippians 1:21, Romans 8:35-39, Hebrews 13:13-14, Revelation 14:13, 1 Corinthians 2:9.

I. E. Kutumov
Karelia-Sosnovsk
January 4th, 1936

PART IV: APPENDICES

The Vins family (1975): From left: Alex, Natasha, Nadia, Lisa, Jane, Lydia, Peter

I. APPEALS FOR GEORGI VINS' RELEASE

The following letter shows the sufferings of the third generation of the Vins family, who are already following in the steps of their parents and grandparents—

To: A. N. Kosygin, the Kremlin, Moscow
N. V. Podgorny, the Kremlin, Moscow
Copies to: Council of Churches of Evangelical Christians-Baptists
Council of ECB Prisoners' Relatives

In violation of the Constitution of the USSR and of international conventions on human rights, our father Georgi Petrovich Vins has again been illegally arrested for his religious convictions and his work in the church.

For thirteen years, our father has constantly been subject to persecutions from the authorities. He served a term of imprisonment from 1966 to 1969, from which he returned with his health seriously undermined. This new arrest causes us to fear for his life. We do not want to see our father posthumously rehabilitated like our grandfather, Pyotr (Peter) Yakovlevich Vins who was sentenced for his religious convictions and tortured to death in the camps, but later rehabilitated.

Our whole family has been suffering persecutions for many years now. Our grandmother, Lydia Mikhailovna Vins, served a term in the camps from 1970 to 1973 because she campaigned for our father during his imprisonment and for other believers who had suffered repressions. Our mother, Mrs. N. I. Vins, was dismissed from her job in 1962 because of her religious convictions and for some years, she was unable to get work anywhere. She is now working, but not in her own profession.

The repressions also affect us children. Natasha Vins was illegally dismissed from work on January 9th, 1974. During a preliminary conversation, the senior doctor of Kiev Hospital No 17, Khryapa, declared that he would find a pretext for dismissing her, since religion and medicine were incompatible. Petya Vins [Georgi's son] has finished the tenth form [i.e., he is now seventeen—Translator's note] but cannot find work anywhere.

All these actions against our family are an attempt to annihilate us. Our father's present arrest is impermissible, and if you do not release him immediately, we will take all possible steps, beginning with an appeal to all believers, telling them what has happened.

We have full reason to suppose that he is in bad health. All responsibility for his life and continued imprisonment rests with you. If our father is nor released and if measures are taken against him in prison which endanger his health, then we want to inform you and believers throughout the world that our whole family is fully resolved to die with him.

Natasha Vins
Petya Vins
Liza Vins
Zhenya Vins
April 18th, 1974

TO THE INTERNATIONAL LEAGUE FOR RIGHTS OF MAN

From Lydia Mikhailovna Vins,
ul. Sosheuko, ixb, Kiev, USSR

I ask you to take whatever measures you can to free my son, Georgi Petrovich Vins (born 1928), who has been in prison in Kiev for six months for his religious beliefs.

The prosecutor's office which has been handling the investigation told us that he is to be charged under articles 138/II, 187/I and 209/I of the Ukrainian Penal Code (corresponding to articles 142/II, 190/I and 227/I in the Russian) and that there may be a charge also under article 214 of the Ukrainian Penal Code (209 in the Russian).

My son was elected by Evangelical Christian-Baptist believers to the Council of Evangelical Christian-Baptist Churches. In accordance with the laws of our country, the authorities were informed about this; nevertheless, he was subjected to persecutions and in 1966, he was arrested and sentenced to three years.

After his release in May 1969, my son continued to serve in the Council of Churches. According to the law, ministers of the church are not obliged to take up secular work. However, as soon as my son was released, the authorities began to demand that he get a job, notwithstanding even the fact that three years of imprisonment had so damaged his health that after release he had to undergo two operations. He still hadn't fully recovered from his time in the camp and from the two operations when they demanded that he get a job; in December 1969, he was suddenly sentenced to a year's forced labor [i.e., obliged to work at a certain place while living at home—Translator's note].

As a minister of the Council of Churches and of the local church, my son sometimes had to make journeys to other churches, and he began to do this in his free time. The authorities forbade these journeys, they forbade him to attend prayer meetings, and several times the police detained him at prayer meetings in his own church.

In December 1969, he was called to the prosecutor's office. In the summons, it stated there was a fresh charge against him under article 209 of the Ukrainian Penal Code (227 in the Russian)—as it turned out later, for a sermon he gave at the wedding of two members of our church. It was stated that the sermon contained appeals for anti-social activity. We have a tape recording of that sermon, and we can make it available to you if necessary.

After receiving the summons from the prosecutor's office, my son informed the authorities that he could not carry on his Christian ministry under such conditions and that he was transferring to full-time Christian ministry. An all-Union search was launched for him.

In March 1974, my son was arrested in the Urals and is now in prison in Kiev.

Article 227 of the Russian Penal Code (209 in the Ukrainian) says: "'The organization or leadership of a group, whose activity is carried on under the guise of the preaching of religious doctrines and the fulfillment of religious rituals, and is connected with the causing of harm to citizens' health or with other violations of citizens' personality or rights, or with motivating citizens to refuse social activity or the fulfillment of civil obligations, and also with the enticement of minors into this group:—is punishable by imprisonment for a period of up to five years or exile for the same period, or by corrective labor for a period of up to one year."

According to article 227 of the Russian Penal Code, the period of imprisonment is up to five years or alternatively exile, but according to article 209 of the Ukrainian Penal Code and in some other republics, they can give up to five years' imprisonment *plus* five years' exile.

This article began to be widely applied to believers of our denomination from 1961. Sentences under this article were not only completely unfounded in law, but they were absurd, and from 1964, they virtually stopped applying it. This was a time when the persecutions were slackening, but in March 1966, the decree was adopted about the reinforcement of article 138 of the Ukrainian Penal Code (142 in the Russian);

and article 187/I of the Ukrainian Penal Code (190/I in the Russian) was adopted. After this, believers began to be sentenced under these articles, chiefly under article 138 (142). The believers were not guilty of violating these articles either, and they wrote to the authorities about this frequently. Now, they have again begun to apply article 209 of the Ukrainian Penal Code because under articles 138 and 187/I, they can only sentence a man to three years' imprisonment, but under article 209 they can give five years' imprisonment and five years' exile. Thus, under this article, they can deprive a man of freedom for ten years. This is the only reason why they have begun to apply article 209 of the Ukrainian Penal Code (and corresponding articles in other republics).

My son is charged under three articles of the Ukrainian Penal Code: 209/I, 138/II and 187/I. He is charged as a minister of the Council of Churches. As we were told in the prosecutor's office,

Lydia Vins at 69 and Georgi's son, Peter (19)—during one of Georgi's prison terms

the charge is based on the "Fraternal Leaflets" [the bi-monthly bulletin of the Council of Churches—Translator's note], letters and appeals of the Council of Churches to the believers.

These "Fraternal Leaflets" and letters of the Council of Churches contain nothing illegal. You can assure yourselves of this if you look at all the materials involved in the case. I beg you to investigate this matter and help in the release of my son. Please do something immediately because the investigation on the case has ended, and they may even conceal the day of the trial from us.

Yours sincerely,
Lydia Mikhailovna Vins, mother.
September 29th, 1974

TO THE AMNESTY INTERNATIONAL ORGANIZATION

From Lydia Mikhailovna Vins,
ul. 11-b, Kiev 114, USSR.

A few days ago, I sent you a letter asking you to petition for the release of my son, Georgi Petrovich Vins, born 1928, who has been in prison in Kiev for six months for his religious beliefs.

He is to be charged under articles 138/1 II, 187/1 of the Ukrainian Penal Code, 209/1 of the Ukrainian Penal Code (142/1 II, 190/1 and 227/1 of the Russian) and the procuracy investigator said he may also be charged under article 214 of the Ukrainian Penal Code (209 of the Russian).

The investigation in this case has now been finished, and the trial could take place in the very near future. Therefore, I appeal to you again and ask you to send your representative immediately, since the trial may begin very soon indeed without our being informed in advance.

I also ask that your representative should have a meeting with my son G. P. Vins and request that all the materials of the case against my son be made available to your committee!

Yours sincerely,
Lydia Mikhailovna Vins, mother
September 29th, 1974

TO THE WORLD COUNCIL OF CHURCHES, AMSTERDAM

I ask you to intercede for Georgi Petrovich Vins, the well-known religious figure, the Baptist, who was elected by his fellow believers as Secretary of the Council of Evangelical Christian-Baptist Churches.

Vins, like other members of his family, has several times been arrested and subjected to other illegal persecutions. Recently, he has been compelled to hide from threat of another arrest. In March 1974, Vins was arrested in Kiev and charged with vagrancy. Protesting against this arbitrariness, he has already for more than four months been on a hunger strike which is threatening his life. The trial is expected in the coming weeks, and he is once again threatened with a prison sentence.

Vins enjoys enormous authority and love among his fellow believers. By interceding in his defense, you will be helping all the Evangelical Christians-Baptists who have now been persecuted for many years by the authorities in the worst traditions of religious intolerance of the Middle Ages and of the Tsarist authorities in the time of Pobedonostsev, in the 1890s.

The arrests, breaking ups of prayer meetings, fines, discrimination in schools and at work, and, as the height of inhumanity, the taking away of children from their parents—all this is the lot of the Baptists and to one degree or another of many other religious groups who are inconvenient to the authorities (Uniates, Pentecostals, members of the "True Orthodox Church" and several other groups).

These illegalities demand the intervention of the world-wide public. Freedom of conscience is an individual part of freedom as a whole. Honest people throughout the world should defend the victims of religious persecutions wherever these take place—in tiny Albania or in the vast Soviet Union.

Andrei Sakharov, Academician
Moscow
September 11th, 1974

TO THE WORLD COUNCIL OF CHURCHES, TO AMNESTY INTERNATIONAL

At his forthcoming trial in Kiev, Georgi Petrovich Vins, the General Secretary of the Council of Evangelical

Christian-Baptists, will be charged under article 209/I of the Criminal Code of the Ukrainian SSR: "Infringement of the person and rights of citizens under the pretext of fulfilling religious rites or under other pretext."

This article has recently begun to be used against Baptists. Apparently, the authorities are attracted by the long term of punishment which is allowed under it: five years' imprisonment, plus five years' exile—more than under other articles previously used against Baptists.

What citizens' rights has Mr. Vins infringed, and whose rights? Certainly not the rights of those several thousand Baptists of the Soviet Union who signed an appeal to the authorities demanding Mr. Vins' release. Apparently, the charge will be constructed on the basis of the fact that Mr. Vins was not working in the service of the state. From this will be indirectly drawn the conclusion that he was living on the means of believers and, in this way, infringing their material rights.

However, in the first place, it is obvious and well-known that the church puts no compulsion on believers to contribute money. And in the second place, how can the authorities make such charges when, for their devotion to God, believers are fined thousands of rubles, all their religious literature (in fact any text which contains the word "God" is confiscated during hundreds of house searches and destroyed, the music and texts of the psalms are confiscated, musical instruments are destroyed, prayer houses are razed, parents have their children removed from them, and the road to any education beyond secondary school is barred to young believers?

The authorities cannot be reconciled with the fact of the existence of the Christian church, whose servants do not follow the directions of the bureaucrats of the Committee for the Affairs of Religious Cults. The fact of the authorities' struggle with the free church, including the helps of article 209/I of the Criminal Code of the Ukrainian SSR (there have already been more than ten trials m 1974), shows that the authorities are grossly infringing the generally accepted rights of believers while cynically pretending to protect their rights.

A. Sakharov
G Podyapolsky
S Kovalyov
T. Velikanova
22nd Octobct 1974

When Georgi's son, Peter, visited his father in Yakutsk prison (1977)

II. A PERSONAL REPORT FROM LYDIA VINS ABOUT THE TRIAL OF HER SON

February 24, 1975

Before I say anything about the trial, I want to say that we are very small people. We have done what we had to do from our youth until today. And the Lord has done great things: in the midst of great dangers and persecutions. He has caused it to happen that "we were considered as dead and behold we live." By His mercy, we have remained alive. And if we should speak about all the sufferings, then it is a story of *all* our people, of our Christians. As one of our songs says, "Whoever has come through struggles and tears." We are very small people, but the Lord has done great things not only through our sufferings, but through the sufferings of all His children who have been particularly faithful to Him for many years and especially in the last decades.

The hardest thing among all these sufferings, especially when you are in camp or in prison, is to realize that you are alone. That everybody in the whole world has forgotten you. And then the Lord is with you as the most faithful friend; and the realization that God's children were praying always revived us, brought us back to life and gave us new strength. Many who have been in prison have testified that they felt people's prayers and they knew not simply those days when they were prayed for, but the actual hours. This is the testimony of more than one prisoner. It was the same with me, too. And it was the same with my son who said at the trial, "I felt the prayers of God's children, and these prayers gave me strength and brought me back to life." We are wholeheartedly grateful first to the Lord for His faithfulness and also to the Christians of the whole world for their prayers. At those times when it was very difficult, in those moments when it seemed that everything was finished, just one thought or one word that someone was praying for us was able to encourage us and bring us back to life, and we were able to continue on our path.

I am very moved by the many prayers that have been made for us, and I am not surprised that my son, when he went, so to speak, through the fire, when he was under attack, still felt very calm, very courageous, very decisive. When I saw him during the trial, tormented and pale, with sunken eyes, I thought: *he hasn't slept for nights.* The trial lasted five days. But when we parted, he said, "I was able to go to sleep peacefully every night. It was a very great mercy of God. It is surely due to the many prayers of God's children." It was the same with me too. When there had been a prayer day, especially after a Sunday, and everyone expected that I would be unable to get up because of my state of health, to everyone's amazement, I did get up and walk; and I knew it was only because of the prayers of God's children. And it was only through those prayers that God gave me life and health and strength, so that I was able to leave imprisonment unharmed, to the amazement of all the atheists.

Of ourselves, we do not deserve these things. But we are so happy that we can represent our whole suffering brotherhood. If people pray for us, care for us, speak up for us, then they have done it for all. They have done it for those who are resolved to remain true to the Lord until death, and there are more than a few thousand such.

Now I want to describe the court situation in a few words. The trial was kept secret from us. When we learned about it, and on that account, wrote to the government that through Voss we had got A. Haerem as our defending lawyer, they called me in specially and spoke to me very politely (although normally they are always very rough) saying that we should accept an atheist to make our defense. We refused. We said it would not be very nice to invite someone else before telling the one who had already been asked. And that is what happened. This lawyer, Alf Haerem, remained our defense lawyer throughout. And every time my son was supposed to answer a question, he would say, "I'll answer that question when my defense lawyer Alf Haerem is here, or he'll answer himself."

Well, to tell everything that happened at the trial would take a long time. Also it would be very difficult and painful. Briefly, I can say that it was not a court tribunal—it was an act of violence. And it is difficult for me to describe the external circumstances or even the contents of the trial, for they kept it secret from us. But the Lord enabled us to learn of the day of the trial. The building was surrounded by strong army forces, and it was simply impossible to get through. This was true not only for the believers or anyone else, but even for his family. During the trial, we managed with great difficulty to get into the courtroom. Very many hindrances had been set up. But we have no time to describe all the minutiae of this. Everybody was pushed away from the building to the other side of the street, and Christians and those who wanted to attend the trial stood out there for days on end, in frost and cold, waiting till the trial ended.

So the trial began, and he was asked whether he had any refusals to the court. The first question affected the lawyer, an atheist state official. My son rejected him and said he had agreed he could not defend him. Then we were invited to say what the situation was regarding the advocate from Norway. I handed in a statement. The advocate was willing to come, but he had not been given an entry visa. Then my son rejected the whole court presidium on the grounds that: 1) It is a one-sided atheist court. It is not I who am on trial, but the whole ECB Christian faith. The Bible, the Gospel, our whole movement is on trial; 2) The investigation had taken place with extreme violence, with the use of physical and mental terror. The investigation had not been conducted by state lawyers but by the KGB. One of their workers had threatened him over a period of two months, and there he is in the fourth row, on the fourth chair at the end, and his name is ____. [Georgi] went on to say that a man had been put in his cell who over a period of two and a half months threatened to strangle and kill him. Thus, he was unable to participate in the investigation. The court rejected this accusation.

He then stated that he would not participate in the trial and listed eighteen points. The first point requested the court to admit an advocate, e.g., Alf Haerem, as a believer. The second request was that a scientific and Christian investigation be prepared with the participation of a Christian lawyer. Since we do not have any such in this country, it must be representatives from other countries. For in the atheist experts' findings, several chapters of the Bible were described as anti-state and even criminal. He said, "in this way, the court confirmed that it is not directed against me. My friends and relatives should understand that I do not ask for a lawyer on my own account, but in order to justify and defend our whole brotherhood and our faith, what it is based and built on, since the whole world accepts it, just as the Bible is accepted worldwide."

His requests also included the formation of a special commission to be composed of members of the leadership of the KGB, of the department for religious affairs, and representatives of the Council of Prisoner's Relatives, to investigate whether accusations put forward in his name from the whole brotherhood were false. He also requested that the tribunal investigating his case should ask from Moscow a review of the number of Christians imprisoned between 1929 and 1945 and how many of these died in imprisonment. The same for the period 1945-1974. Also how much Christian literature was confiscated, including Bibles, New Testaments, and hymnbooks? How many Christians were excluded from higher education on various pretexts? How many prayer houses were destroyed between 1929 and 1974? How many Christian parents were deprived of their parental rights and other questions relating to the position of Christians?

The president of the court was partial in his cross-examination of the witnesses. None of the witnesses requested by my son were permitted to enter the court. During cross-examination of the witnesses, particular questions were asked, geared toward the intended sentence. After this type of cross-examination, he was asked to state his opinion. He said he would only make a statement in the case of a thorough investigation in the presence of his defense lawyer Alf Haerem. He would make no statements in these conditions. But he did give an explanation, saying:

"I insist that here in our country a campaign of annihilation is being waged against Christians. Since you have refused to obtain the facts, I can tell you that from 1929 to 1945, 25,000 Christians were imprisoned and 22,000 died in the camps. From 1945 to 1974, 20,000 were imprisoned and 6,000 were excluded from higher education. Since 1929, 10 million books have been confiscated. These are the main points, indicating that even today Christians are being physically annihilated in the camps and prisons.

"I could be at home today. From the first day of my imprisonment onward I was invited to collaborate with the security police with the Council of Churches; then I could go home to my children. But I refused. Now I know that the Lord permitted it, and I accept from His hand anything He wants."

Then the experts spoke. In fact, the whole of the experts' findings was not read out loud. My son was accused of:

Falsifying Soviet reality. There was no persecution here. His story "Faithfulness" had been published in various news releases of the Council of Prisoners' Relatives and in other places. This history of Christianity was directed against the state; it was criminal and contained lies. In this story, he described the life of several leaders of the Christians (Baptists) in recent times, their sermons and letters. Then there was the "Family Chronicle" about the fate of his father, his mother, his uncle, etc. In the experts' findings, they had accused him of acting against the state and appealing for rejection of the legal order, but they had not found this proven. The president of the court suggested since they had heard the testimony of the witnesses, could they not improve this and write that such appeals had been recorded on tape? They agreed.

Then my son was given an opportunity for defense. He said, "My defense should be conducted by Alf Haerem. But now I leave my whole case with my Lord Jesus Christ." Then the state counsel spoke. A sentence of five years of prison camp and five years of exile in Siberia, with confiscation of property, was proposed. Then he was given a last word. But since he did not take part in the trial and his requests had been rejected, he replied, "The last word belongs to my Lord Jesus Christ, who said: I am the Alpha and the Omega, the beginning and the end." That was all.

The sentence was announced the next day. When it was read out to him and they asked, "Have you understood?" he said, "Yes, Glory to Jesus Christ."

Then Christians gave his relatives flowers—roses, carnations, narcissi. Until then, the flowers had been concealed under their clothes. These flowers were thrown to him. His son took them and threw them, saying, "Daddy, these are for you and your bravery." His wife threw flowers to him, saying, "You have won this trial." Also his daughter. The whole room clapped. When the flowers were thrown, everyone fell silent. The whole room was full of people with invitation cards. They applauded and laughed. His daughter Natasha climbed on a seat and said, "No, Daddy, the church will not die [a reference to one of his poems], just as the love of Christ does not die. With Christ, you are free in prison. And freedom without Him is prison."

Usually he was led out last, but this time first. He went out carrying the flowers and saying, "Greetings to all friends." By this time, there were more than 500 believers outside the building and about 200 who had come by bus and tram. They were all waiting for this moment and holding bouquets of flowers. But he was secretly led out another way. Then all the believers removed their headgear and began to sing. It was very moving. The group of 500 sang—everybody sang. Everything was still; no one moved. Then I came out with my grandson, leaning on his arm. He took off his cap, as at a funeral. They opened up to let us through and we made our way back home. But the day before all the young people had gone through the back entrance to the place where his prison car stood. And he heard them singing the song: "For the faith of the Gospel . . ." Police came up, but nothing could be done until he was taken away. This was the trial.

Four days later a reunion was permitted. His wife and son met him, only two persons were permitted and the three small children. They did not allow me or his daughter to go in. The reunion took place through a glass door or wall, and there were telephone booths through which they spoke to him. The conversation was certainly overheard; they couldn't discuss anything special. He said, "I didn't want to hand in the appeal." But we asked him to do it. Not to get him off, but to demonstrate that a higher instance would pass the same sentence. We don't know whether he handed it in or not; this is being concealed from us. Today (Monday) a parcel was taken to him that he would be in deepest Siberia. He asked for very warm clothing.

But what will the Lord do now? We are full of anticipation. I recall that the whole world, all Christians, are concerned for us. We do not deserve it. And this flag of victory belongs first to the Lord and then to the quiet, unnoticed martyrs who go silently, many times leaving their large families behind, who prefer to suffer and die rather than deny the Lord. We should talk about these too. Now

I ask you to tell all Christians that the greatest thing they can do is pray. If anyone can make an appeal for him, as the Lord permits, we are prepared to accept anything.

And the suffering of our whole brotherhood is expressed through my son's name and all our family. People should not speak about us only, but about all the Christians here, so that they can live freely, if that is the will of our Heavenly Father. And tell this particularly to those who were directly involved in the case, who made a great effort, both brother Voss and others who wanted to take part, who were ready to attend the trial. This is wonderful. We never thought that our desire to have a lawyer from outside would mean so much for Christians of the world and would reveal the truth.

I forgot one important thing. Concerning the matter of a defending lawyer, we were given a meeting at the end of October, where he asked for a Christian defense. That took them by surprise. I was meeting him again after four years of separation . . . When I was released, I was followed by unknown people for five months. They watched every step. I had no chance to go anywhere because they were after me. They watched my flat. When he was arrested, this surveillance was lifted. That's why I wasn't able to see him for four years.

I met him again in the prison regarding the matter of a defense lawyer. When it was time to leave, we prayed. We had been told beforehand that we must not speak about any matter but that of a defense lawyer. That was in order that he could not speak about how they had treated him and what his situation was now. But when I left, he said, "Mama, bless me." That was all. So we prayed. I blessed him and prayed over him. We did no wrong. But at the trial he said, "After the reunion with my mother, I ate and drank nothing for twelve days." He wanted to say what they did with him, but they wouldn't let him. They ordered him to sit down, and I don't know what happened. But at the trial, he said he was only able to get up two months out of ten. That's all. For clarity, I would like to repeat the accusations against my son:

◊ Violation of the law on religious cults which involves: Ban on all missionary activity, inviting young people into the church, Christian education of children. These are the main points of his article. It is regarded as a criminal article of the USSR.

◊ Falsification of Soviet reality through news and information about the persecution and imprisonments of believers.

◊ Violations of rights of citizens, e.g., any sermon calling for conversion or more precisely, any missionary activity. This is the strongest article, which also refers to damaging citizens' health. "Under the pretext of religion, violence is practiced on a person's body and the moral life is destroyed." In contrast to the other two, which entail three years' imprisonment, violation of this article entails ten years: five years' labor camp and five years' exile (Siberia).

For a second sentence, as was the case with my son, prisoners receive an increased punishment: the first parcel of food is permitted only after two and a half years; during these first two and a half years, he may not receive any parcel. Meetings: once a year. Correspondence: one or two letters a month. These explanations must be added in order to understand why my son and also other believers were sentenced under a convenient pretext. This article has become a welcome basis for sentence because it gives the longest term of imprisonment.

III. VINS' APPEAL REJECTED

May 8, 1975

Further details concerning the case of Georgi Vins, the reform Baptist leader, have been received at Keston College (Centre for the Study of Religion and Communism). The information is taken from the letter of March 26, 1975, which Lydia Vins, Georgi's mother, addressed to the Human Rights Committee and Amnesty International.

On March 5th, the Vins family delivered a letter to the Supreme Court of the Ukraine in which they drew attention to the illegality of his trial. Vins had himself already appealed to the Supreme Court against his sentence. The court heard his case on March 6th and rejected the appeal. The family was not informed that the hearing had taken place, nor were they told of the decision until March 19th—despite almost daily inquiries. The fact that Vins was in a hospital during this time was also "painstakingly hidden" from them.

The family has also been refused a copy of the official verdict by the Kiev City Court. The judge, a man named Tyshel, claimed that they only wanted a copy in order to send it to the CIA. He described the family as "enemies of the people" and "hoodlums." Now they are being shadowed, and the house watched.

Lydia Vins appeals for help in opening a reexamination of the case with the participation of a Christian lawyer and representatives from the Supreme Court of the USSR and Amnesty International.

According to an official note of March 25th sent to Lydia Vins, her son is to serve the rest of his sentence in the Yakutsk Autonomous Republic (Eastern Siberia). His health is reported to be "satisfactory."

EPILOGUE

Georgi Vins spent a total of eight years in the Soviet prisons, imprisoned for his faith in and service to Jesus Christ. Much of the content of the book you have just read was smuggled out of the USSR and put into the hands of Keston College in England in 1967 and eventually U.S. publishers.

In 1979, then U.S. president Jimmy Carter arranged a dramatic prisoner exchange with the USSR: one religious (Georgi Vins) and four political Russians in USSR prison camps for two convicted spies. Part of the terms of the exchange was that Georgi's family members would be allowed to join him in America, which they did and resettled in Indiana. Georgi's mother, Lydia, passed into glory in 1985 at the age of 78.

Once in America, Georgi started a ministry to assist the persecuted church in his homeland. His eldest daughter, Natasha, actively participated in this ministry alongside her father and later her husband Alexander. When communism was disbanned in the USSR in 1991, the Vins' family traveled to Russia many times over the years to share the Gospel.

In 1998 at the age of 69, Georgi went home to be with the Lord after a short illness with cancer. His wife, Nadia, passed away in 2004. Natasha carried on her father's work with Alexander until 2019 when she too passed away from cancer.

You can read more about Georgi Vins and his family in *The Gospel in Bonds* and *Moscow Express*, both in republished editions.

For those who are taught by Christ
To subdue the elements by strength of faith.
The sun of victory will shine
Through the gloomiest clouds. G.V.

ENDNOTES

1. Andrew Brown, "Peter Wiens and Georgi Vins: Faith Strengthened by Trial" (Mennonite Brethren Historical Commission, No. 60, Fall 2016, https://mbhistory.org/profiles/wiens-vins).

2. According to certain information, B. was killed after the war during the Ashkhabad earthquake of 1948.

3. The Decemberists were a group of Russian officers who took part in an unsuccessful liberal uprising against Nicholas I in December 1825.

4. Boyars were a class of independent landowners in early Russian history.

5. Omitted passages of Lydia Vins' defense speech might still be found in another copy of the speech in the files at the Center for the Study of Religion and Communism: they concern other Baptist believers.

6. In the Ukraine alone, of the 2,000 Evangelical Christian-Baptist communities in 1946, the authorities had closed 800 prayer houses by 1960.

7. Georgi quotes a short list according to the brochure "Our Baptist Principles," written and published by Peter Vins in 1923 in the Far East.

8. *The Baptist*, No. 2, 1925, p. 1.

9. Printed here with significant abridgments.

10. The Molokans or "milk-drinkers" were a Russian sect who rejected the Orthodox emphasis on ritual and claimed the right to live according to the Scriptures.

11. Stone of help.

PHOTO CREDITS

Photos on the following pages are from the personal collection of Georgi Vins' daughter, Natasha Velichkin; used with permission from the Vins' family trustee: pages 14 (top photo), 17, 25, 30, 55, 56, 95, 208.

Page 12: From alamy.com; used with permission.

Page 14 (bottom photo): From the Keston Center for Religion, Politics and Society; used with permission through Baylor University.

Page 66: Public domain; from Wikipedia; https://commons.wikimedia.org/wiki/File:Talkessel_von_Werchojansk.JPG.

Page 71: Taken from http://zarubezhje.narod.ru/mp/M_838.htm.

Page 72: Scanned from the cover of the now-out-of-print book, *Konshaubi: A true story of persecuted Christians in the Soviet Union.*

Page 90: From https://www.primetour.ua/pictures/fck/image/art_Luk_prison_.jpg; in public domain.

Page: 135: Wikipedia: https://en.wikipedia.org/wiki/Balthasar_Hubmaier; in public domain.

Page 136: Ukrainian Evangelical Theological Seminary. Library of UETS; https://digitallibrary.usc.edu/asset-management/2A3B-F18AOLPG.

Page 149: https://clever-geek.imtqy.com/articles/7550072/index.html; Georgy Ivanovich Shipkov.

Page 174: Taken from https://vk.com/wall-27569095_2022024?lang=en.

Page 180: Painting of Russian peasant, 19th century. From alamy.com; used with permission.

Page 196: From the Keston Center for Religion, Politics and Society; used with permission through Baylor University.

Page 202: Ibid.

SOME OTHER TITLES BY LIGHTHOUSE TRAILS PUBLISHING

BY GEORGI VINS

The Gospel in Bonds: 8 Years in the Soviet Gulags—Imprisoned for His Faith, $13.95

Moscow Express and Other Stories From Russia, $12.95

BY OTHER LIGHTHOUSE TRAILS AUTHORS

A Time of Departing
by Ray Yungen, $14.95

Castles in the Sand **(a novel)**
by Carolyn A. Greene, $13.95

Color, Communism, and Common Sense by Manning Johnson, $12.95

Faith Undone
by Roger Oakland, $14.95

For Many Shall Come in My Name
by Ray Yungen, $13.95

Foxe's Book of Martyrs
by John Foxe,$14.95, illustrated

How to Prepare for Hard Times and Persecution by Maria Kneas, $13.95

How to Protect Your Child From the New Age & Spiritual Deception
by Berit Kjos, $14.95

In My Father's House
by Corrie ten Boom, $13.95

Let There Be Light
by Roger Oakland, $13.95

Muddy Waters
by Nanci des Gerlaise, $13.95

Seducers Among Our Children
by Patrick Crough, $14.95

Stories from Indian Wigwams and Northern Campfires
Egerton Ryerson Young, $15.95

Strength for Tough Times
by Maria Kneas, $11.95

The Good Shepherd Calls
by Roger Oakland, $14.95

The Other Side of the River
by Kevin Reeves, $14.95

Things We Couldn't Say
by Diet Eman, $14.95, photos

Trapped in Hitler's Hell
by Anita Dittman with Jan Markell, $13.95, illustrated, photos

Up From Slavery
by Booker T. Washington, $13.95

War Against the Saints
by Bill Randles, $10.95

For a complete listing of all our books, DVDs, and CDs, go to www.lighthousetrails.com, or request a copy of our catalog.

To order additional copies of:

Three Generations of Suffering
Send $14.95 plus shipping to:

Lighthouse Trails Publishing
P.O. Box 307
Roseburg, Oregon 97470

For shipping costs, go to
www.lighthousetrails.com/shippingcosts.htm or:
($3.95/1 book; $6.00/2 or more books)
You may also purchase Lighthouse Trails books from
www.lighthousetrails.com.

The bulk (wholesale) rates for10 or more copies is 40% off the retail price.

For U.S. & Canada orders, call our toll-free number: 866-876-3910.
For international and all other calls: 541-391-7699
Fax: 541-391-7697
Three Generations of Suffering, as well as other books by Lighthouse Trails Publishing, can be ordered directly through Lighthouse Trails.

For more information on the topic of this book:
Lighthouse Trails Research Project
www.lighthousetrailsresearch.com

You may visit Georgi Vins' website at: www.georgivins.com.

Lighthouse Trails has a free bi-weekly/monthly e-newsletter and a quarterly subscription-based 40-page print journal. Visit www.lighthousetrailsresearch.com, or call one of the numbers above to sign up for the free e-newsletter or to subscribe to the print journal. ($14/year for U.S. | $22/year for CA | $34/year for international).